FOUNDATIONS OF KINGDOM LIVING

By

Chaplain Jessie Czebotar

Requests for information should be addressed to: Illuminate The Darkness PO Box 10443 Fargo, ND 58106.

PRELUDE

I have come to conclude that out of all the callings the Lord gives, none is more intense than that of a son of God called to Spiritual Warfare to fulfill his duties as a warrior and king. I have never known a time in my life where I have not been right behind our Lord and Savior out on the front lines in the spirit world. I was born and raised in the heat of the battle, trained beside the Lord while in the enemy's household. Those who have heard my testimony know of my bloodline family that sat at the very top ruling seats within Satan's System. This book is not meant to scare you. It is meant to draw you closer to the Lord, equip you to understand your calling as a Warrior in His army, and prepare you as the Bride of Christ. There are difficult and hard truths I will bring forward in this book. By the end, you will have full understanding of your calling, your purpose, and your heavenly duties in the Kingdom of God.

WE ARE THE BRIDE OF CHRIST.

"Let us rejoice and be glad and give the glory to Him, for the marriage of the Lamb has come and His Bride has made herself ready." Revelations 19:7

Never forget…WE ARE A KINGDOM OF PRIESTS.

"His Kingdom is not a matter of talk, but of power." 2 Corinthians 4:20

WE ARE THE SONS OF THE LIVING GOD

"For all of creation waits in hopeful expectation for the revealing of the sons of God." Romans 8:19

Get ready for the Holy Spirit's power this day! (Prayer taken from my Prayer journal dated July 19, 2022.

"O Lord God Almighty, who is like You? We wake to command this day and time to work on our behalf. Thank You for giving the FULLNESS of Your strength, power, might, and authority. I bind those things to us this day and loose a demonstration of Your Holy Spirit's power. Loose unto us tongues that we may speak boldly of Your Gospel and of Your Resurrection power.

I command this day that we may walk in the fiery furnace with You and not get burned. Release to us commanding fire tongues by which to express the authority You've given us to govern and rule and reign with You. We loose those tongues from above now unto Your Body and Your Bride.

Bind Your Words before our eyes, our foreheads, upon our lips and tongues, and upon our hands. As we speak Your Words, let them go forth with a demonstration of Your power. As we ask for Your will to be done, perform the acts immediately. Let them proceed forth from Your mouth and go out to accomplish exactly what You have purposed them to do. Release to us the tongues of commanding fire that raise the dry bone armies. Let us testify as eyewitnesses to Your glories, splendors, and majesties across the world.

Release to us the blood of the Lamb and the word of our testimonies so that we may overcome the evil one in the heavenly Courts above and in the earth below. As we intercede and cry out, let the voice of the blood be heard that speaks on our behalf. Loose our ears that we may hear the voice of Your seven-fold Spirit. As we hear, so give an added portion of obedience to do Your will.

Release to us strength, endurance, and might. Lord, grant us an added measure through our long days. Bear us up on eagle's wings. Let us stand firm and steadfast, continuing to press on, even unto old age. Thank you for the keys to the Kingdom so that we may bind and loose. We ask for these things in the Name of our Lord and Savior Yeshua Ha Mashiach.

Walk uprightly in your blessing, dear brothers and sisters."

Table of Contents

1

GET READY

"And then you shall see the Son of God coming in the clouds with great power and glory." Mark 13:26

If one is to start discussing one of the most intense and difficult topics of all time to tackle, I guess there is no better place to start than with a story that shares my heart. The first four years of my life were beautiful. They were filled with childhood wonder, discovery, playfulness, and laughter. I was born into a loving home with good parents. My father's side of the family are what I classified as Holiday Lutherans, meaning they attended Church on the Holidays, but otherwise, the only other religious thing they ever did was fish. It was in the loving arms of his mother and sisters that I was first nurtured in the States of Minnesota and then in Wyoming.

Wyoming was the land my heart loved. I would wake up bright and early. Jumping with excitement, I would drive my grandmother crazy as I begged to be let outside. She was a clever woman and not quick on the draw that early in the morning. She had to find a way to work around my morning exuberance, so, she would quietly go to her kitchen cupboard and stand on her tippy toes to reach for her finest China teacups she kept on the top shelf. She would set that beautiful dainty cup on the cupboard and then say, "Jessie, if you are good and quiet, I will pour you and I a cup of coffee. We can sit down together and drink it on the couch. Then after our coffee, you can go play outside." At the word coffee, she had my full attention. It was considered the forbidden treat. Upon hearing the words, I would get so excited. Of course, I wanted that one thing my parents would never let me have. I learned to sit quietly for the first 20-30 minutes of the morning with her.

I wrestled as I was forced to hold all my energy bundled-up in one spot. I attempted to overcome the challenge by focusing all my attention on that little teacup. My mind was always racing with a multitude of thoughts. It was like a massive rubber band ball with too many thoughts going in too many directions. There were way too many things to think about just to focus on one. But this morning routine taught me to give way to just picking one thing to think upon. That little practice began to teach me to take hold of one thought at a time and to sit with it, to think on a deeper level about things. No matter how long I looked at that beautiful teacup tracing all the flowers and design details in my mind, eventually, my thoughts went to the place I could not wait to be in.

My grandmother's backyard was the epitome of my life. As one came out the back door into the fenced yard, there was a big, flat, grass yard that was dried and brown from the heat of the sun. The tint-colored grass was separated by a chain-link fence that sat in front of a steep hill that went up the road behind the house. The hill was covered with cactus and tall, wild, unmanaged, prairie-type grasses. The first yard was filled with all sorts of wonders. To the right was the old-fashioned silver metal clothesline pole. I fully believed at age three that I could fly and I was obsessed with trying to prove it with that clothesline. I would stand by the main pole with both hands on it. I would start to run as fast as my little legs would take me and then I'd let one hand go and around I would twirl until my bottom hit the ground. My grandmother knew the truth, I knew the truth, yet she delighted in watching me have fun.

Behind the clothesline was my favorite tree in the yard, the Lilac tree. It stood about 6-7 feet tall and was big, round, and lush with light-colored purple clusters of flowers. I would part the lush brush and find my way underneath the bottom boughs and lay on the dirt. Gazing upward, I would lie there smelling the fresh floral scent that filled the space. This was my hiding place away from the noise, the hustle and bustle of a house filled with boy cousins. It was the only place I could bring my questions to God. To the far left of the yard was an old, wood, boxed-in sandbox and one lone tall apple tree. This was my work area. I grew up in a family of religious fishermen. So of course, all good fishermen need to have their night crawlers. I was fascinated with not only night crawlers but with all varieties of bugs. My grandmother used to tease me about my adventures and started calling them my "Bug Hunts". I was allowed to put all the bugs I found in a quart glass jar each day. I could carry them around, look at them, but at the end of the day, I had to release them back into the great outdoors.

Early in the mornings I would rise and as soon as my grandmother and I had finished drinking our coffee, I would be running outside with that glass jar to go dig in the dirt under the apple tree. I also liked to climb up as high as I could in the apple tree. It became a place I loved and hated. We had a red-headed neighbor boy who was a bully named Billy. He would chase me and my cousins around the yard until we climbed up the tree to get away from him. The first few times he ended up pouting when we would not come down, but then he began to climb up after us. We would climb higher to get out of his reach, but Billy would pursue us until he got a hold of us by the ankles. I would feel his strong hand take hold, I remember looking down at his sinister eyes and freckled face. He would get a gleeful smirk on his face right before he whipped me out of the tree onto the ground. I remember hitting the ground so hard that it knocked the wind out of me. I will never forget the fear of not being able to take a breath. This was the first place where the spirit of fear started to try to get a hold of me.

When we are little, we see clearly. We see, we hear, and we feel in the spirit world; however, we don't know what to do with what we are experiencing. There were so many supernatural moments I experienced that left me feeling clueless in how to react. I remember one morning, my siblings, my cousins, and I were sitting at the kitchen table eating corn flakes. My two-year-old brother stood up on his chair and pointed out the window. His eyes were dead locked toward a certain place in the back yard. It was not the yard he was looking at though. It was a place in the air. And as he intently gazed, he suddenly spoke slowly with a clarity and certainty that shook me, "Jesus is alive. Right there. He's right there. He is alive." As I followed to the place he was pointing, I caught my first glimpse of Him. There was a man blazing like fire with the sun shining in all its radiance behind Him. Later, we experienced this same vision of the Lord while we were in a restaurant. And I personally would experience the Lord appearing this way during a significant event in my childhood. The sight of Him brought me to the first time I had experienced the Presence of the Lord.

2

LITTLE ARROWS OF BROKENNESS

At that young age of three, the Lord heard all my heart's response towards Him. He saw my struggles and challenges. Health has always been something I wrestled with. I was born with Eustachian tube issues that affected my hearing and I had to get my first set of tubes in my ears at age one. After that, I was plagued with non-stop ear infections. I was blessed to have an excellent Ear Specialist named Dr. Horn. He was an elderly, old-fashioned hometown doctor. He had a kind heart and combined his work with playful stories and games that made office visits a fun childhood experience. Dr. Horn captivated my attention and had a unique way of drawing out my mischievous sense of playfulness.

In the corner of his office stood a little round table with a bright, yellow tablecloth draped over it. Little wood chairs that were painted white complimented the child-sized table. Every time I came for my monthly visits, he would have the table set when I arrived with a plate full of lemon sandwich cookies and a little tea pot of warm tea. He would invite me to come and sit at the table with him. As he reached for the elegant containers holding sugar and cream, he would wiggle his white mustache back and forth. In a funny prim and proper voice, he would ask me how I wanted my tea. Usually, I replied that I wanted one cube of sugar, but sometimes he would plop two in there, cover his mouth with his hand and say, "Oops, guess you need some extra sweetness today." We would both laugh. As we drank tea and cookies, he would look in my ears.

My ears were just one more thing that slowed me down. I was not a fan of sitting quietly, nor of having to sit still. Yet, for several hours throughout the day, I had no choice but to just rest. Every day after lunch, my grandmother would put a pillow on one side of the couch. I would lie down on my side and she would put two drops of antibiotics in my ear. I had to lay on my side for thirty minutes. During that time, my overactive mind had to be kept busy. I learned to do quite a lot while making sure I kept my head in the sideways position it had to be kept in so the drops stayed on my ear drums. After thirty minutes, I would roll to the other side and the process began again.

The ear drops always amplified the sound of everything in the room. I could not distinguish sounds nor the direction they came from because they sounded blurred and loud. One morning, there was this huge BAM that filled the living room. It startled me so much I jumped off the couch in terror and ran to get my grandmother in her room. She came out of her room holding my hand and reassuring me everything was ok. She said, "Jessie, it's Springtime. The cocky male robins are out and they like to fly and hit the windows. Come, let's see what's going on outside." She opened the front door and there lying in the dirt in front of the living room window was a robin. He was lifeless and still. As we approached his body, I watched as my grandmother picked him up and held that motionless body cupped in her hands. Slowly, she began to move her hands back and forth in a rubbing motion. The robin's beak began to open and close. “There, you see. He’s not dead. Do you want to touch him?” She extended her hand holding the robin out to me. As I reached my index finger out hesitantly to touch him, suddenly, the robin popped up and stood on her hand. He turned and looked at me. Then, just as quickly as he came, he flew away and was gone. Although this moment turned out good for the robin, I remember I was left with a feeling of fear. I wanted to understand, what happens when one gets their breath knocked out? Does one’s breath always come back? Or can one die when their breath gets knocked out? Little by little the spirit of fear began to invade my thoughts.

3

THE FOUNDATIONS OF KINGDOM LIVING

"Man does not live by bread alone, but by every word that proceeds from the mouth of God." Matthew 4:4

Most churches do not teach that the reason strongholds of sin are present in our lives is because of the access we give to the idols and demonic spirits behind them. Things happen in our lives where the doors to these idols and spirits are opened. Instead of knowing how to close those doors, we allow access to remain. The Lord's desire is for us to open our eyes to see the access points or footholds we allow the enemy to have in our lives. It's important to realize the truth...we ALLOW or give permission for the enemy to use the footholds. The Holy Spirit is saying, "No more!" We are a people that belong to Him. Now is the day that He is moving us to deeper waters. Whenever the Lord is about to move me to a deeper place, He often will stimulate thoughts that lead me in direction and strategy on how to get where He is leading. It's time for fierceness. Tear down the idols and strongholds in your life so that the Spirit of the Living God can move.

What I love about the topic of Kingdom Living is that we are learning to live the new life that has been bought, purchased, redeemed, and raised up. All too often it is easy for our attention to be drawn to our health issues and the things that are wrong in our lives. As I began to seek out the Lord's healing for health issues I was struggling through, He led me to certain Scriptures to think upon that speak to certain areas of the body that need health. It occurred to me that there is a strong possibility that many health issues are due to idols and strongholds.

Up until now, no one has ever broken down for me a full understanding of the Kingdom of God versus the enemy's kingdom; nor how each operates. I believe this is key to understanding how idols and strongholds operate in our lives. I also have never had anyone break down the full extent of diagnosing issues of the spiritual body through the manifestations of illness occurring in the physical body. I believe these foundations are important for us to comprehend so that we can experience complete healing. In the next few chapters, we will learn about the new life we have in Christ. I will explain Kingdom Living, the Kingdom of God, and how the Kingdom of God and the realm of power can be accessed.

We are living in a time where the Holy Spirit is about to break forth with signs, miracles, and wonders that will manifest through our spiritual gifts and disciplines. One of the spiritual gifts that I have is visions. A vision means that you see with your spiritual eyes the things taking place in the spiritual realms. These things can be past, present, or future. In 2022 the Lord began to show me a vision of a table right in the center of the battlefield. When I asked Him why it was there, He led me to Psalm 23 where it says, *"He prepares a table for me, in the presence of my enemies."*

One night while in prayer, I saw this vision so strongly. In the vision, I saw a table sitting underneath what looked like an open tent outdoors. As I continued to pray, the Lord told me to notice the details of the vision. As I looked deeper, suddenly I could hear the wind blowing and I heard the sound of curtains flapping in the wind. The sound was so distinct and powerful. Then I noticed the beautiful, fine, lace tablecloth that covered the thick, oak table. The lace pattern was so delicate and intricate. As I gazed more deeply, I saw a wrap-style couch around the table that was gold and silver in color with an intricate design. I noticed that there was no food on the table. I asked the Lord why there was no food. He responded by showing me another vision. This one was of the time He visited Abraham under the oaks of Mamre. *(Genesis 18)* The Lord said to me, "Abraham prepared a meal for Me." As I began to read the chapter, verse 6 caught my attention.

> *"So, Abraham hurried into the tent to Sarah, and said, 'Quickly, prepare three measures of fine flour, knead it, and make bread cakes. Abraham also ran to the herd and took a tender and choice calf and gave it to the servant, and he hurried to prepare it. He took curds and milk and the calf which he had prepared and placed it before them (the Lord and the Angels); and he was standing by them under the tree as they ate." (Genesis 18:6-8)*

Accessing the Heavenly realm begins by understanding your identity and your relationship with the Lord. Do you know who you are? Starting in childhood, we learn to define ourselves by words. We are a child, a son, or a daughter of our parents. We learn to define who we are by our culture, our environment, surroundings, our likes and dislikes, our age, illnesses, and other worldly factors. Even growing up in a church culture, we learn to define ourselves by biblical terms such as, Christian, believer, unbeliever, son/daughter of God, child of God. These labels are made to make you feel safe, secure, and good. Did you catch that? These labels are intended to make you feel a certain way. But how many of us really feel we are who our labels claim that we are?

As a child, I grew up in a "Christian" environment. I remember hearing Scriptures that told me I was part of God's family and that I had new life in Him. I believed it. However, there was one problem; I did not FEEL it! Sunday after Sunday, I attended church wondering if others felt that way, but I was too scared to ask. The first time I heard someone else admit that they struggled with the same insecurities I felt was when I was working at the Veteran's Mental Health Facility as a Chaplain.

I will never forget the first time I met Roy. He had been a Christian his entire life and had attempted to live a godly life. He was married and had served several years as a Deacon in his Church. As I came into the tiny, glass room to meet with Roy, what I saw before me was a broken man who had been trampled in the miry muck by the enemy. He could not even lift up his head because of his shame from attempting to take his own life through suicide. In desperation, Roy proceeded to tell me about his Christian life and what had transpired that led to the suicide attempt. The issue surfaced as he began to speak about God's promises from the Bible that he believed he had. I will never forget the look on Roy's face as he spoke the words, "Chaplain, if I have new life, how come I have never felt it." His words were like a blow to my own chest. The truth was that I believed the same things the Bible promised, yet I also struggled my entire life to truly feel it.

I remember seeking the Lord for the words to say. What does one say to address this issue? As I sought the words, the Lord brought to mind my own struggles. At the root of this issue was the fact that I grew up in churches that taught salvation, yet not one of them had ever left me feeling the assurance of that salvation. Every Sunday I would go to church and when the pastor gave the altar call, I was the first to be found running up to the front, confessing my sins and begging the Lord to forgive me and secure my eternal state. Why was this fear of the loss of salvation something that I struggled with? It's because we are taught to base our faith on works rather than securing our faith so that it rests in Christ's work alone. Many churches teach that if you are in sin, you will lose your salvation.

> *"The Lord said to Moses, "Whoever has sinned against Me, I will blot him out of My book." (Exodus 32:33)*

> *"Then they will cry out to the Lord, but He will not answer them. Instead, He will hide His face from them at that time because they have practiced evil deeds." (Micah 3:4)*

> *"For I tell you, unless your righteousness exceeds that of the scribes and Pharisees, you will never enter the Kingdom of Heaven." (Matthew 5:20)*

> *"Do you not know that the wicked will not inherit the Kingdom of God? Do not be deceived: Neither the sexually immoral nor idolaters nor adulterers nor male prostitutes nor homosexual offenders nor thieves nor the greedy nor drunkards nor slanderers nor swindlers will inherit the Kingdom of God." (1 Corinthians 6:9)*

They use these verses to teach that sin defines our current state of being and that dictates our eternal position. Therefore, we are led to believe that any sin we are in gives us an automatic eviction from being in Heaven. This belief structure puts us on shaky ground. So how do we move from being on shaky ground to standing upon a firm foundation? We have to let our faith rest in the power of God rather than in the wisdom of men. It is only when we fully accept that there is nothing we can do with regards to our sin and eternal state that we will be free to know the truth. Scripture tells us, "*But you know that he appeared so that He might take away our sins. And in Him is no sin." (1 John 3:5)* I love this verse and believe the English language does not do it justice. In English, we translate it "He takes away". The Greek word **αἴρω** (aírō) taken from ***ἀείρω*** (aeírō, "to lift, remove") implies that the taking away is done with a violent grasping and removal. So, it would better read as, "*He violently seizes our sins with force and removes them from us."* When does this violent removal occur? It happens the moment we die with Him. Romans 6:4 states, "*We were therefore buried with him through baptism into death in order that, just as Christ was raised from the dead through the glory of the Father, we too may live a new life."* The moment we believe, we are buried with Him and raised to new life.

This is your moment. If you have struggled with insecurities in your salvation or identity in Christ, it is time to firm those things up. Make some time to go before the Lord. Enter into His Presence and don't leave until you have that certainty that your salvation rests in His work alone. O how precious the work that was done on the cross for us. How precious the blood that secures our salvation. Take further time to secure your identity. In the next chapter we will be looking at who we are in the Kingdom of God.

4

WHAT IS OUR KINGDOM IDENTITY?

"And you know without a doubt that Jesus was revealed to take away our sins, and there is no sin in Him. Anyone who continues to live in union with Him will not sin. But the one who continues sinning has not seen Him with discernment or known Him by intimate experience." 1 John 3:5-6 The Passion Translation.

The solution to every problem comes through a Word from the Lord. I love The Passion Translation of 1 John 3:5-6 because it shows us clearly the answer to the problem. How do we break free from our insecurities in the areas revolving around our salvation and our identity in Christ? The breakthrough comes by knowing Him and by having intimate experiences with Him. The breakthrough happens when we realize that we are not bound to the sin nature anymore. Every moment is a moment of choice. You choose in those moments who you will serve. Will you choose to serve the fleshly nature and continue to go on sinning? Or will you choose this day to serve our Lord and Savior Jesus Christ? Will you get up every day and take the time to have moments of intimacy with the Lord? When is the last time that you experienced closeness with the Lord, the kind of closeness that leaves you satisfied. The Lord is alive. You have a relationship to tend to. If you have not been tending that relationship, today is the day that change needs to happen. Today is the day you stop holding back and withholding from a God who loves you so very much.

Do you know how to nurture love in your relationship with the Lord? Scripture says, *"I pray that out of His glorious riches He may strengthen you with power through His Spirit in your inner being, so that Christ may dwell in your hearts through faith. And I pray that you, being rooted and established in love, may have power, together with all the Lord's holy people, to grasp how wide and long and high and deep is the love of Christ, and to know this love that surpasses knowledge—that you may be filled to the measure of all the fullness of God." (Ephesians 3:16-19)* Our relationship with the Lord starts by "grasping" the depths of His love for us. There are two requirements in the action of grasping. It is interesting to note the components involved in these actions that lead to them happening.

First, you must be "*strengthened with power through the Holy Spirit in your inner being*." This first action must be released in order for the second to occur. How do we do this? You can only be strengthened by the Holy Spirit if you are making yourself available to spend time with Him. What do you know about the Holy Spirit? The Word says He is our Counselor. That implies we can talk to Him and He will listen and help us process and walk through our problems. We will never know how He can help until we let Him. So, there is a surrender that is involved in the relationship. Many of us are good at giving but we struggle to receive. You have to be able to receive before you can be strengthened with the Holy Spirit's power. Once we have received the power of the Holy Spirit, then we are strengthened with that power through the Holy Spirit in our inner being which gives way so that Christ may dwell in our hearts through faith. Assurance is a process that, like a plant, must be grown in order to be harvested. What we are accentuating here are the steps to assurance in salvation and the process to firming up the foundation we stand upon. So how do we firm up the assurance of salvation?

When I was a child, I experienced the loss of someone very dear to me. He was a boy my age and had been chosen as my occultic training partner and protector in the Luciferian Brotherhood which I simply call the "System". I thought the families I grew up in were your typical Christian homes. My dad's side were Lutheran and like most Lutherans, they attended Church on the Holidays and whenever they felt led to. My mother's side were devout Catholics and attended mass regularly. However, my mother's side of the family had a dark secret. Their Christian life was a cover in order to hide their dark involvement in the Luciferian Brotherhood.

There were many horrific things I witnessed and endured with a little boy who was my training partner in the System. What I want to share here is that there was a moment in my life where the enemy tried to deceive me. In the midst of our trauma, the Lord made me and that little boy a promise. That promise was that we would be delivered out of this occultic System. We believed the Lord and over the next six months we began to make plans of escape. In our innocence, all we could see ahead of us was the hope of the day we would get out. We did not know how or when. We were so filled with hope that we could not even see that all our plans were just that, our plans. The night of October 31, 1984, the Lord put into motion His plans.

That night, my family took me to a haunted house. I was there with other family members who were part of the System. It included my Proctor (the woman who was training me and raising me up to succeed her in her position in the Luciferian Brotherhood), and two young aunts who were five and ten years older than me. At one point in the house, the paths parted. My Proctor and aunt who was five years older than me went one way and I went with the older aunt towards the other hallway. The hallway was pitch dark, but suddenly the lighting and atmosphere changed. The hallway lighting turned to a red color and a thick fog rolled in. I remember feeling her grip tighten around my hand as she stopped and took my arm and drew me closer to her side. I could hear the fear in her voice as she said, "Jessie, I know you're scared. It's ok. I'll carry you." In my spunk I replied, "I'm not scared." She scooped me up in her arms awkwardly while saying, "I'll carry you anyway." Little did we know that the Lord's powerful shift awaited just moments ahead. As we crept forward, we saw a skeleton in a cage to the right side of the hallway. As we neared, we saw the skeleton's arm extended out into the hallway grabbing for whatever it could touch.

My aunt attempted to skirt past it, but it was too late. As we tried to squeeze past, the skeleton's arm got stuck around my ankle and we could not get it off. There was no one else in the hallway and after several attempts to remove the skeleton hand from my ankle we resolved to yelling for help. The staff finally came. After several attempts to remove the skeleton's grasp, they realized that they also were not able to get the hand off my foot. So, my aunt stood there holding me while they called in some maintenance guys. When the maintenance guys came, I noticed right away that they were individuals I have never seen before. I believed they were not part of the System. I took the opportunity to break the code of silence and I began to tell them all about the System with the hope that they would help me to get out. I remember the main maintenance guy staring at me with bewildered eyes. Looking back, I wonder what he was thinking hearing the words that came from my mouth. I'm sure he was thinking, "Who is this kid? Is she part of the haunted house?"

As I continued to speak about the evils my family was engaged in, my Proctor came around the corner and heard what I was saying. That night, the System staged the death of my training partner. I remember that I went to bed like usual only to be awakened sometime in the middle of night. I was dragged down the stairs by my Proctor. As my feet hit the cold front steps, I remember time stopped as though it was put on pause. I heard the blaze of the fire. My gaze turned to see my training partner's house that was down the road on fire. My heart sank and I began to run towards his house. The neighbors and firemen were gathered outside. As I got closer, I saw my training partner banging on the second-floor window. He was yelling that he could not get out. I went to run for the front door and was grabbed by my arms by two strong firemen. I began to kick and wrestle trying to get free from their grip, but they lifted me by my arms up higher in the air and held me like that kicking and screaming. I watched as my training partner moved back from the window. We heard his voice and that of his grandfather and brother crying out for help and I remember the moment those voices stopped. All that followed was a deafening overwhelming sound of the fire blazing and a smell of burning flesh.

When I believed that he was dead, a great depth of anger was stirred in my heart towards the Lord. I still loved the Lord and passionately had the desire to serve Him. But, I was angry that He had allowed the death of my training partner and that He had not fulfilled His promise to get us both out. In my anger, I responded to the Lord by making a prayer request that I knew the Lord could never answer. I asked the Lord to raise my training partner from the dead. When the Lord did not answer that prayer request, in my anger, I set it as a place marker between me and the Lord. It stood as a reminder to testify to my anger in the matter. It would always be that "thing" between me and the Lord.

There were several times in my life where the Lord afforded me moments to deal with this anger. But, I did not want to. I wanted to hold on to it. When I refused to deal with it, I would feel guilt and regret. "Why did I have to continually try to break the silence? Why couldn't I just keep my mouth shut? If only I had kept my mouth shut, maybe my training partner and his family would still be alive? Maybe I had ruined God's plans for us and if I had kept my mouth shut, we would have gotten out." The thoughts often reeled through my mind over the next few years. Maybe these whirling thoughts and anger were exactly what I wanted to hold onto. The occult had taken the life of my training partner (or so I believed) because I had chosen to break the vow of silence and had told individuals outside the System that my family was in the occult and did horrible things. Oh, how the enemy likes to use these little things we don't want to surrender to the Lord and he capitalizes upon our wounds that come from sins, regrets, fears, mistakes, and hurts we have experienced. Satan uses them to cause us further damage physically, spiritually, and emotionally. As we attempt to hold onto those wounds, they begin to fester. The deep festering infection takes all sorts of various forms. It can turn into guilt, shame, oppression, depression, lack of trust, withdrawing, isolation, and withholding in love.

What if that which we allow to fester is only a tactic the enemy uses to keep us from entering into the Lord's Presence and allowing Him to forcefully remove from us the sin, the baggage we choose to carry, and all that should not be in our lives*? If this is so,* *why do we allow the enemy to continue to capitalize upon our wounds when we could be healed?* Let me say that again. Why do we allow the enemy…to continue to capitalize upon our wounds! Do you want to be healed? If you truly want to be healed, there is only one place you can go. You must let go of all that is holding you back and you must run straight away into the arms of Jesus proclaiming, "Lord, here I am, take it all from me. I want to be made well." I often have found that the greatest works God allows us to partake in come at times when we are broken, weary, and unexpecting. To continue to move forward in our spiritual growth, we must take a look at who we are in Christ. Who are we?

> *"At midnight the cry rang out, 'Behold, the bridegroom! Come out to meet Him." (Matthew 25:6)*

Before we can live, we must understand who we belong to. We have been bought with the precious blood of our Lord and Savior Jesus Christ. We have died with Him and been raised to life in Him. But what does it mean that we have been raised in Him? Who has He raised us up to be? One bright summer day when my children were little, I got them ready and we went to hike a trail in nature. As we walked along the dirt path, my daughter noticed fuzzy caterpillars. I fondly remembered when I was five and had collected caterpillars at school and I wanted her to have the same fond experience. So, we collected them and made nice, little cozy homes for them in jars with a long stick, grass, and leaves. Easy peazy, right? Big sigh. Well, nothing turned out like I had remembered. The caterpillars ate lots of leaves and grass and crawled up on the sticks like they were supposed to and hung upside down. But after that, everything went wrong. Instead of forming a chrysalis, these caterpillar's bodies turned black, shriveled up, and their heads fell off. I remember thinking, "What in the world did I do wrong?" I was going to throw them away, but my daughter reminded me that I told her it would take about 6-8 weeks for the butterflies to hatch. She begged and I gave in to her pleadings.

Would you believe to my surprise 6 weeks later, out of those black, shriveled-up bodies with no heads, three of the most beautiful blue-winged butterflies emerged. I remember asking the Lord, "How can this be?" A year later, He brought me back to this experience and showed me the rest of the revelation. It was a powerful vision that secured my faith. He showed me how I died with Christ, and I saw that I had been raised with Him. I fully grasped in that moment that it is His work. His death is so complete. Everything of our old sin nature dies and, in that moment, it is separated from us just like that black, shriveled-up body is separated from the caterpillar. Everything that it was and formerly had been dies. Yet, in that moment of transformation, the Lord raises us up into new life. With a breath, we are raised with Him into that new life. *"Therefore, we have been buried with Him through baptism into death, so that as Christ was raised from the dead through the glory of the Father, so we too might walk in newness of life." (Romans 6:4)*

It's time to throw your struggles and hindrances to understanding these truths aside. If you have asked the Lord to forgive your sins, the work is complete. His work is complete. He has been faithful to finish it. Do you believe this? There is nothing you can do to earn your way into His Presence. He's made the way for you to come so that you may reign with Him. 2 Timothy 2:11-13 states, *"It is a trustworthy statement: For if we died with Him, we shall also live with Him; If we endure, we shall reign with Him; if we deny Him, He also will deny us; if we are faithless, He remains faithful for He cannot deny Himself."*

I want to bring out an important truth from 2 Timothy 2:11-13. I have experienced many churches that use this verse to emphasize their point that one can lose their salvation. I do not believe that is what this verse is saying. The Greek for "if we deny Him" means that if we disown, reject, or denounce Him. It does not translate that if we sin, He will disown us. It is very specific. And it has to do with your belief. Those that believe in Him shall have eternal life. However, those who choose to not believe in Him shall be disowned. A word of caution. We know that sin shall not enter into Heaven. Therefore, we must be found in Christ and be holy as He is holy. How do we do this?

"He who believes in Him is not judged; he who does not believe has been judged already, because he has not believed in the name of the only begotten Son of God." (John 3:18) What name is that? *"If you confess with your mouth, 'Jesus is Lord', and believe in your heart that God raised Him from the dead, you will be saved." (Romans 10:9)* Does this give us the right to be found in sin? Not at all. The sheer fact that He extends us grace should be enough to bring us to our knees in thankfulness. Do we really think enough upon what it cost Him to take our sins from us? We each need to truly take the time to reconcile our deaths in Christ. At the same time, we need to really spend time considering our new life. He has raised us from the dead. There is power in the resurrection. The resurrection is the key to accessing the Heavenly Realm of power.

"With great power the apostles continued to testify to the resurrection of the Lord Jesus. And God's grace was so powerfully at work among them." (Acts 4:33) This is such an important piece to understand that I must ask again, do you understand that you have been raised to new life and have full access to the fullness of Christ? Colossians 2:9 says, *"For in Christ all the fullness of the Deity lives*

in bodily form, and in Christ you have been brought to fullness. He is the head over every power and authority." It is this understanding of our resurrection with Him that unlocks the authority and power we have received to rule and reign with Him both on this earth as well as in the one to come.

So, who are we? I believe our identity in Christ is broken down into three main positions within the Kingdom which are described fuller in Scripture. His Word states that you are 1) the Bride of Christ, 2) you are a Kingdom of priests, and 3) you are the sons/heirs/warriors of the Living God. Each of these positions come with duties that we are to perform. Each has an aspect of governance. This book focuses on breaking down the position of being the Bride of Christ. These positions are Kingdom jobs. I do not believe that our duty to perform these jobs occurs only once we have passed from this world to the next. I believe that we are stewards of this Kingdom living now! If that is the case, then we have Kingdom duties and jobs to perform. Do you know what your duties as the Bride, the priest, or the son are? Are our duties just here in the physical realm? Do you have spiritual duties that you are to perform now? In order to perform duties in the spiritual realm, you must have access to it. Do you currently have access to the Heavenly realm and the throne room of God? When is the last time you used that access? Does the Word teach us about our duties in both places and what our duties entail?

The Bible uses a great deal of imagery and pictures to paint in the readers minds spiritual truth about who we are. The question is, do we really comprehend how those pictures connect to our relationship with Christ and our role within His Kingdom and in the Heavenly battle? This is where we must begin before we can step out onto the battlefield as mighty warriors. We must comprehend our identity and understand the authority and power that we have been given in our Kingdom positions. Each position is different and has various components of Kingdom governance. Living has everything to do with our knowledge and understanding of these truths.

5

THE BRIDE OF CHRIST

"O my dove, in the clefts of the rock, in the secret place of the steep pathway, let me see your form, let me hear your voice; for your voice is sweet, and your form is lovely." Song of Solomon 2:14

Let's start by looking at what His Word says about being the Bride. What does it mean that "we are the Bride of Christ", and what does it have to do with overcoming the evil one? Typically, the Bride imagery is not associated with battle imagery. Back in 2009 the Lord began to reveal the connection between the Bride and war to me. I sat quietly in the hospital room attentive to Pam as she spoke. She was a paraplegic and had a wound in her buttocks that was about a hand-length deep. For over a month, doctors and the burn unit surgeons had attempted to get the wound to heal up with their best methods and medicines, but to no avail. Her crippled-up body was wedged by pillows in her wheelchair to keep all pressure off the wound. Physically she did not look comfortable, but there was a glowing smile on her face and her spirits were uplifted as she spoke while looking out the window. "I had the most beautiful dream last night of my wedding."

I was a little shocked at first to hear her words. I knew if doctors did not figure something out soon, she would die. As I gazed at her glowing face, her curly, brown hair and brown, dove-shaped eyes radiated from her smile. I was drawn into her vision and her words captivated me, "I wore the most beautiful glistening white gown that flowed so gracefully as I walked down the aisle. My hair was pulled back and I had a crown of white lilies upon my head that shone like pearls. I was standing and walking down the aisle on top of flower petals." Then she smiled even bigger as she said, "I saw him, I saw the man I will marry." Tears began to flow down the side of her cheek as she said, "And I praise God for such a lovely sight."

I will admit there was a part of me that was skeptical. I knew the depth of her wound. I had been privy to the team of doctors and surgeons who discussed her care plan and were on the brink of finding no cure for Pam's healing. This skeptical part of me wondered if God would heal her or if this dream she had was a vision of her future marriage to Christ. There was something about it that had drawn my heart to Him. I long for the day when I will see His face and be presented before Him as His beautiful Bride. Yet, at the same time, in complete contrast, I do not typically want to think about The Day of the Lord.

Coming out of the occult, I dreaded the thought of the wrath of God that will be unleashed on that day against His enemies. For about 40 years, I have cried out and wrestled with the Lord for those who are held under Satan's bondage to receive mercy. Yet, the Lord has said that now is the time of His righteousness and with it comes His justice and His wrath. A few years back, the Lord brought me to the epitome of this wrestling over the matter between His mercy and wrath. In a vision, He showed me a little candle in my hand and said it was called mercy. It was such a small light. He told me to bury it in the altar of coals in His throne room and that it is time to declare His judgements upon the wicked. There was no more wrestling after that. His Word shall be accomplished. There is so much yet to be revealed. Who can understand what the day of the Lord's wrath will be like? It is not just a day of judgement; it is also a day about Christ and His Bride. That is why we do not need to fear His wrath. Because as the Bride we are called to rule and reign with Him and to judge with Him.

> *"The seventh angel sounded his trumpet, and there were loud voices in heaven, which said: 'The kingdom of the world has become the kingdom of our Lord and of His Messiah, and He will reign for ever and ever." (Revelation 11: 15)*

> *"Let us be glad and rejoice and give honor to him: for the marriage of the Lamb is come, and his wife hath made herself ready." (Revelation 19:7)*

For the better part of my life, I had a very difficult time understanding the love that God has for me. Love for me was experienced in togetherness. I would feel the love of God in the presence of others. But when things happened to those individuals, when they went away or were taken away, I struggled to feel love because I felt all alone. I wonder how many feel that way. You believe the Lord is real, but still struggle when you don't feel His Presence. In 2010, the Lord began to reveal to me visions about the Bride of Christ. One night, as I was doing my devotions, the Lord sang me a song. I wrote the words I was hearing as tears poured down from my eyes.

BEAUTIFUL BRIDE SONG

"Beautiful Bride, won't you keep your light shining

Search for Me in the clouds, very soon I am coming

Watch in the night, and you'll see when I come riding

You're lovely, dressed in white

Set apart just for Me

When I take your hand in Mine

Then I know you are with Me

Together we shall sing, in perfect harmony

I shall laugh as we dance, and the angels join around us

I will know you are Mine as you put your hand in My hand

You shall be called My Bride

You shall go forth in My Name"

Even after the Lord sang the song, I struggled to understand the concepts He was trying to show me. The Lord knew my inner turmoil, so He decided to assure my heart again the very next morning. It was Sunday and I was excited to go to Church because we had some Missionaries from Uganda that our Church supported coming to speak that morning. They had been married that year and decided to share the story with all of us. The two of them had met serving separate warring tribes in Uganda. June, being a single female Veterinarian, had been adopted by her tribes' chief as his daughter for her protection. So, when Wesley asked for her hand in marriage the chief asked him to pay the chief bride's dowry of cows. The number requested was almost an impossible number to attain given the average salary someone of his standing made. But with help from Churches that supported him, he finally came up with the dowry price. After sharing this Wes became silent and looked around towards each face in the service as he said, "After paying such a price there was no way I was not coming for my bride. I paid many cows for her, but Christ paid with His own blood for you. You better believe there is no way He is not coming back to take His Bride unto Himself."

The power in his words impacted my heart even more as he showed videos of his coming for his bride. He stood in the midst of warriors: tall, dark, African men jumping and hollering with spears in their hands. They looked like they were ready for war not for a wedding ceremony. These fearsome warriors began to pull women from their housing structures looking for the sole white woman who was to be Wes's bride. When they finally had her, she was brought into the midst of the fearsome warriors, knowing only that her husband to be was somewhere in the midst of them, too. Our God is the King of a Heavenly Host of Angels. What an awe-inspiring day that will be when He comes for us.

Why do I share these stories about the bride? I believe this is a big piece of our identity in Christ that we have lost, especially for men. Men have a hard time understanding the importance of the Bride analogy and how it applies to the body of Christ. We must "sure up" our identities and our salvation. It starts by understanding that you are His Bride. You belong to Him. He is very fond of you and in love with you. Maybe it's easier to embrace if we see the Bride as a position that wields great authority in God's Kingdom. He has given His Bride authority to rule and reign with Him. When we know who we are, then we can understand what He has called us to do. I believe the Bride is made to be front and center on the battlefield. The Bride on the battlefield? I know you are asking, "What does the imagery of a Bride have to do with the battlefield?"

6

THE AUTHORITY OF THE BRIDE'S VOICE

"I will give you the keys of the kingdom of heaven; whatever you bind on earth will be bound in heaven, and whatever you loose on earth will be loosed in heaven." Matthew 16:19

These last days are the days of great harvest. The war takes place on a spiritual plain that we cannot see. The battlefield is overflowing with a golden harvest of wheat that is ready to be gathered. On one side stands our enemy. He hurls insults and taunts the army of God trying to get them to turn away from gleaning the fields. The Devil strives to pluck as many sheaves of wheat that he can for he is only a thief that "*seeks to steal, kill and destroy*." *(John 10:10)* The Lord stands tall on the other side and shouts, "*I have come that they may have life, and have it to the full." (John 10:10)* I can almost see the enemy's sneering jeer as he taunts, "Where is this salvation the Lord promised? Why does He tarry?" The Lord has spoken, and His promise will not fail, "*The Lord is not slow in keeping His promise to come...instead He is patient with you, not wanting anyone to perish, but everyone to come to repentance*." *(2 Peter 3:9)* The beautiful testament to these truths about the Bride are found in the Book of Ruth and the stories of permissions given to Ruth to glean the fields.

What are our duties and responsibilities in the Kingdom of God as the Bride within the scope of authority given to us? This scope of authority is powerful and can be broken down into two areas: firstly, the voice of the Bride and secondly, the form of the Bride. In the Song of Solomon, we see the eyes of the Groom searching out the Bride. When He sees her, He is captivated. What did He see that captivated His heart and caused Him to love her? He proclaims, "*O my dove, in the clefts of the rock, in the secret place of the steep pathway, let me see your form, let me hear your voice; for your voice is sweet, and your form is lovely.*" *(Song of Solomon 2:14)* The Groom saw the Bride's form and heard her voice. The "voice of the Bride" is something the Lord longs to hear. What is it that the Lord longs to hear? Isaiah 58 says,

> *"Cry loudly, do not hold back; raise your voice like a trumpet, and declare to My people their transgressions and to the house of Jacob their sins. Yet they seek Me day by day, and delight to know My ways, as a nation that has done righteousness and has not forsaken the ordinance of their God. They ask Me for just decisions, they delight in the nearness of God. 'Why have we fasted, and You do not see?' 'Why have we humbled ourselves and You do not notice?' Behold, on the day of your fast you find your desire, and you drive hard all your workers. Behold, you fast for contention and strife and to strike with a wicked fist. You do not fast like you do today to make your voice heard on high. Is it a fast like this which I choose, a day for a man to humble himself?"*

The Lord desires to hear His children to understand that they have a voice that represents His power and might when it is released on the battlefield between His Kingdoms on heaven and earth. How powerful is the voice He has given us. We have His full authority in His Name to bind, to release, to declare, and to proclaim the intentions of His heart. How do we know what to speak? This is a matter of intimacy; we can only speak what we hear the Lord saying. So, in order to know what to speak forth, we must know the Lord's heart and the desire of His will. The Bride can only know this from spending intimate time in His Presence.

Do you see how the covenant position the Bride is in affords access and closeness to the Lord? Not just to enter into His chambers to bring requests, but this access enables us to draw near, near enough to be face to face with the Lord. So close that we speak with Him cheek to cheek and ear to ear. In conversation with the Lord, we learn how to speak forth what we hear.

Isaiah 58 is a passage that stirs my heart like no other for it teaches us how to use our voice. Let's define the authorities of our voice.

1) Binding and Loosing
2) Releasing
3) Declaring
4) Proclaiming

Binding and Loosing

Binding and Loosing is the exercise of one's indisputable Kingdom authority to command either by forbidding or allowing. That which is forbidden is cast off or away. That which is permitted is attached, fastened, or made secure. For example, we are to command that the Word of God be ever before our eyes. *"Fix (Bind) these words of mine in your hearts and minds; tie them as symbols on your hands and bind them on your foreheads." (Deuteronomy 11:18) Again, the Word says, "Do not let them out of your sight, keep them within your heart;" (Proverbs 4:21)* At the same time, we are given the keys to the Kingdom so that we may bind the strongman, that is the Devil. *"I will give you the keys of the kingdom of heaven, and whatever you bind on earth shall be bound in heaven, and whatever you loose on earth shall be loosed in heaven." (Matthew 16:19)* The Lord's promise stands firm when we exercise our authority on earth, it is also accomplished in heaven. *"Truly I say to you, whatever you bind on earth shall be bound in heaven, and whatever you loose on earth shall be loosed in heaven." (Matthew 18:18)*

Releasing

Releasing comes from the Hebrew word "deror". It is used in relation to the Lord's redemptive work of freedom from slavery and bondage. This same word is used by the Lord in His offer to free us from our sins. It's like a door of escape that opens up to release one from bondage. If we were to apply it, release means to "give", to "release", to "remove chains of bondage and the yoke of oppression". We have been given a commission, a task to do for the Kingdom. Matthew 10:7-8 says, *"As you go, proclaim this message: 'The kingdom of heaven has come near.' Heal the sick, raise the dead, cleanse those who have leprosy, drive out demons. Freely you have received; freely give."*

In practice, how does releasing work? As we spend time in the Lord's Presence, He shares His heart, His desires, and His longings with us. He meets our needs. He heals, restores, binds up our wounds, applies healing balm, and forgives our sins. As we receive these blessings from the Lord, we then in turn are to release them to others in need. What the Lord gives to you, you then have the authority and responsibility to give to others. Release is used to break both the chains of wickedness and the yoke of oppression. Why should we continue to live bound or under a heavy yoke when the Lord's righteous justice has been given and with a word, we can get out from under them. He has given us such a great authority. When we speak forth His words, they accomplish the execution of His will. *"Is not this the kind of fasting I have chosen: to loosen the chains of injustice and untie the cords of the yoke, to set the oppressed free and break every yoke?" (Isaiah 58:6)*

Declaring and Decreeing

Declaring is a fine art. Many times, in Scripture we see the word for declaring go hand in hand with decreeing. To declare and decree means to establish or issue an official order. It is a legal term that can be executed or come to pass. There are several conditions that must be put into place to help you understand how to use declarations. Declarations must be issued in alignment with God's will and the person issuing must have the right or authority to issue. In our declarations, we state what we know to be truth that the Lord has made known. As we speak it forth, it is established in the heavens and the earth.

Does decreeing something make it happen? There are two verses many believers stand on when they are declaring and decreeing.

> *"You will also decide something, and it will be established for you; and light will shine on your ways." (Job 22:28)*

> *"Truly I say to you, whoever says to this mountain, 'Be taken up and thrown into the sea,' and does not doubt in his heart, but believes that what he says is going to happen, it will be granted to him. Therefore, I say to you, all things for which you pray and ask, believe that you have received them, and they will be granted to you." (Mark 11:23-24)*

Some use these verses incorrectly by teaching that if you have "enough faith", then anything you speak forth will come to happen. Decreeing is not speaking forth something that is not into existence. Decreeing is simply declaring (speaking forth) what God has already established or set in place. It is not a guarantee that something shall happen, it is speaking forth who the Lord is (His Names) and what He has already accomplished, or what He has said He will bring to completion.

In order to exercise this authority, we must have faith. However, that faith must be aligned with the Lord's will. This is the key. We cannot just make things happen. Only when our faith is aligned with the Lord's will shall we see the word executed and brought forth. The Bride's duty is first to the Lord. Did you catch that? Listen again. The Bride's duty is first to the Lord. Our attention and our eyes are to be set on Him. This is the spiritual discipline of "seeking fast after Him." Scripture says, *"The Lord looks down from heaven on all mankind to see if there are any who understand, any who seek God." (Psalm 9:10) Seeking must be done in faith and when we pursue the Lord in faith, it is rewarded.*

> *"And without faith it is impossible to please God, because anyone who comes to him must believe that he exists and that he rewards those who earnestly seek him." (Hebrews 11:6)*

> *"You will seek me and find me when you seek me with all your heart." (Jeremiah 29:13)*

The Bride is put into a position where she ministers unto the Lord and listens to Him, He shares His heart and the intentions of His will. As He shares, the Bride declares. As we declare, matters are established in the heavens and upon the earth. There will be times as we reason and wrestle with the Lord in prayer over certain matters in our lives that He will allow us to establish our decision by making a rendering in the matter. We see this ordained in the Book of Job *(22:28)* I believe that "rendering a decision" is a most honored reward and should not be taken lightly. It increases as we grow in our faith and the Lord entrusts us with more responsibility. There is only one way to be given the authority to render a decision. It only comes to those who diligently seek Him.

Proclaiming

The last way that the Bride asserts the authority of her voice is through proclaiming. Proclaiming is very different from declaring. Many get the two confused. While declaring is speaking forth what already is, proclaiming is speaking into existence what currently is not in existence. What a powerful perspective that adds to Jesus' words as He stood in the temple of God and proclaimed,

> *"The Spirit of the Lord is on Me, because He has anointed me to proclaim good news to the poor. He has sent Me to proclaim freedom for the prisoners and recovery of sight for the blind, to set the oppressed free, and to proclaim the year of the Lord's favor." (Luke 4:18)*

What do we have the authority to proclaim? I believe Luke 4:18 gives us the formula for proclamations. In this verse, Jesus establishes the matter in the spiritual and physical realms by making two declarations: "The Spirit of the Lord is on Me" and "He has anointed me to proclaim good news to the poor". Out of the declarations flow the proclamations. Because the Spirit of the Lord is upon Him, and because He has been anointed, therefore He is sent to proclaim: 1) the good news, 2) freedom for the prisoners and recovery of sight for the blind, 3) the oppressed are set free, and 4) the year of the Lord's favor. Notice that by making a declaration first, the will of God is made known and the authority of the one giving the proclamation is irrefutable. Why does this need to be pronounced? We are in a war. We have an enemy who is the accuser of the brethren and who has temporary authority here on earth. Luke 4:18 is not just a statement Jesus made. It was a heavenly declaration and proclamation that gave to us the authority to execute His will in the heavens and in the earth. Remember the keys we have been given in the Kingdom. Just as we receive, so we are to give.

Here is where you must make a decision. The Bride's voice cannot be heard nor the power of the authority the Lord has given to her be seen, unless the Spirit of the Lord and His anointing is upon her. Will you take that step today of committing to seek the Spirit of the Lord and His anointing so that you may access the realm of power? The Lord is preparing a feast for His Bride on the battlefield before the enemy, but His Word says that "many are called but few are chosen." *(Matthew 22:14)* Why are few chosen to walk in the position as the Bride and attend the marriage supper of the Lamb? I believe it comes down to willingness. In theory, we all want to be that Bride so that we are in a position to be close to the Lord. This theory is only in our minds and imagination until we choose to put it into practice. The truth is that not many are willing to lay down "their lives" in order to learn how to truly live as the Bride of Christ.

In the Kingdom of God there are layers. Many believers learn the surface layer to Kingdom living which feels very comfortable and nice. It's nice to be a seed planted in fertile ground. This is not where we are meant to stay. The Kingdom of God is comparable to a tree. In order for a tree to grow and bear fruit, it must achieve the depth, the height, and the breadth of all it is capable of attaining. Do you want to bear fruit for the Kingdom of God? Do you want to know the fullness of your identity in Christ and all that the Lord has created you to be? Then you must "*seek first the Kingdom of God and His righteousness, and all these things shall be added unto you." (Matthew 6:33)*

Being the Bride is not a solo job. The concept of the Bride of Christ must be understood as a corporate position. Scripture says that we are the Body of Christ. *(1 Corinthians 12:12, 27; Romans 12:4-5)* A body is made up of many parts, each part having its distinct function. The height, depth, and breadth that we are to live in comes to its fullness when we learn to live and walk in the realm of power together.

7

THE FUNCTIONALITY OF THE BRIDE

"There is one body and one Spirit, just as also you were called in one hope of your calling;" Ephesians 4:4

As the Bride seeks the Lord, He adorns her with beautiful gifts. These gifts are our weapons of warfare and tools that we need in our role and function as a steward and possessor of the Lord's house. *"The weapons we fight with are not the weapons of the world. On the contrary, they have divine power to demolish strongholds." (2 Corinthians 10:4)* As we enter in to abide in His presence, as we seek His face, we shall know His will. Then we are to go out with the Lord to establish His Kingdom on the earth. As we go out with the Lord into battle, we speak forth His will and tear down strongholds of wickedness and break the yoke of oppression over communities and across nations. Carrying a mantel of Esther, the Bride's voice is one that seeks justice for the oppressed and the wicked. As we speak forth justice, we also walk in the spiritual discipline of fasting so that the strongholds of wickedness may be broken and so that the yoke of oppression may cease. Our voice is one that tears down and binds the enemy. With our beautiful voice we begin to take back what the enemy has stolen from the Kingdom of God.

> *"Jesus called them over to him and began to speak to them in parables: 'How can Satan drive out Satan? If a kingdom is divided against itself, that kingdom cannot stand. If a house is divided against itself, that house cannot stand. And if Satan opposes himself and is divided, he cannot stand; his end has come. In fact, no one can enter a strong man's house without first tying him up. Then he can plunder the strong man's house. Truly I tell you, people can be forgiven all their sins and every slander they utter, but whoever blasphemes against the Holy Spirit will never be forgiven; they are guilty of an eternal sin.'" (Mark 3:23-27)*

In 2022, the Lord gave me a powerful vision one night. I saw a woman standing at a city gate. Along the gate were tents that held shops. The woman had gone to a man who ordered supplies for her and requested the items she needed in her shop. She waited and waited and still the supplies were delayed because the man did not think to put the order through. Then a storm blew by and her shop tent was torn. She was unable to repair it because she did not have the supplies she needed. There was a second man who had a shop close to hers. He offered to let her come and share space in his shop, but he had conditions. Next to him was a poor woman. Her shop tent had been destroyed in the storm as well. No one knew that she had just finished years of caring for her elderly mother who had now passed away. She had hoped to sell soaps to make a living, but the storm had destroyed everything. In the vision, the Lord told me that neither of the men were doing what the Lord desired.

The Lord desired that the first man had been obedient and ordered the first woman's supplies. Then she would have been able to do what the Lord called her to do after the storm by ministering to the second woman and repairing both their tents. Although the second man was good, he also was still not doing the Lord's will. The Lord did not desire conditions to be put upon the first woman's work. What He desired was that all involved would display one another's beauty.

The Bride is endowed with the seven-fold Spirit of the Living God. As she wars, she prepares the hearts of the people to make them ready for the coming of the King. Preparation is an aspect of the Bride's form. The Bride prepares the hearts of the people by displaying the form of her beauty. This is not something unique to the Bride. The Lord is all about the business of displaying His beauty and majesties within us. Everything that He does is so others may see that display of beauty. "Preparing" is all about displaying the beauty of the Lord in others to the world. Do we live in such a way that we are preparing things for others so that the Lord's beauty in them may be displayed?

The Lord searches and watches for the form of His Bride. What does this mean? It means He is waiting, searching, and watching for you to show up. Did you ever stop to think how excited the Lord gets waiting for you? I never fully grasped this until I reread the book of the Song of Solomon. The portion I was reading says it is the voice of the Lord speaking. As I read the words of Song of Solomon 3:6, the Lord literally took me my surprise.

"Who is this one ascending from the wilderness in the pillar of the glory cloud? He is fragrant with the anointing oils of myrrh and frankincense-more fragrant than all the spices of the merchant." (Song of Solomon: The Passion Translation)

As I read the words, it reminded me of the Scriptures where both Moses and later Jesus ascend the mountains to have that one on-one time with the Lord. Does the Lord smell the fragrance of us coming into His presence? Does He watch as we ascend upon His holy hill? What does the Bride's form look like? First, her form is spotless and pure and endowed with gifts from the Lord. We are not talking about the outward appearance nor natural gifts being defined as things we are born with and are good at. We are speaking of the endowing of gifts upon the spiritual body that are displayed in the physical world. Our form should be such that others are drawn to God because of what they see in us. Authority is a gift that the Lord endows us with.

"Therefore I, the prisoner of the Lord, implore you to walk in a manner worthy of the calling with which you have been called, with all humility and gentleness, with patience, showing tolerance for one another in love, being diligent to preserve the unity of the Spirit in the bond of peace. There is one body and one Spirit, just as also you were called in one hope of your calling: one Lord, one faith, one baptism, one God and Father of all who is over all and through all and in all. But to each one of us grace is given according to the measure of Christ's gift. 'Therefore, it says, 'When He ascended on High, He led captive a host of captives, and he gave gifts to men.'" (Ephesians 4:1-8)

When I was working at the VA Hospital, I had just had my sixth child. I laugh looking back now, but the VA Hospitals were not set up for working mothers. I was still nursing and needed to have a place to pump bottles every day. The only room that was available was down in the basement right next to the morgue. Not ideal; however, I made up my mind that I would make the best of this situation. The first day I went down, I passed by two offices. The first one was empty, but as I came near the second, a lovely man named Torrance came out to greet me and to inquire about why I was wandering in his neck of the woods.

As I spoke with him, it did not pass my notice that he was wearing a unique necklace with a deer on it. I recognized it as a pagan symbol. So, I inquired, "I could not help but notice, Torrance, that's a very distinct necklace you have on. Does it have meaning to you?" He was not reluctant or ashamed to share that he was pagan, and that paganism was his religion. This little conversation opened the door to many that followed. I called them the "five-minute specials". Sometimes, the Lord works in such mysterious ways. Who would have thought that He would use my need as a nursing mother to meet the needs of a pagan man who was desperate for a glimmer of meaning in life and a miracle.

Every day as I came down to the room, I found Torrance waiting with a big, huge smile on his face. We would take turns talking about all sorts of things that were happening. I needed something to pass my time while I did my pumping so I would bring books down with me to read. The Book I was reading at the time was called "Christ at the Round Table" by E. Stanley Jones. Torrance enjoyed hearing about the missionary who set up round table discussions with all sorts of individuals from various religions in India and the chronicle of their discussions.

As our discussions grew, one day Torrance met me at the door with a downcast face. He proceeded to tell me that they found out his wife had cancer and he asked if I would pray for his wife as she went in for her appointment with the doctors and further testing. I agreed to pray for her. I watched day by day as this man whose office sat right across from the morgue wrestled through his trial. I can't imagine what it was like for him to be in that morgue area, faced with death every day, and then carrying the weight of his own fears that his beloved wife may soon suffer the same fate. It was several months later that Torrance met me at the door across from that morgue once again with a big, bright smile. I will never forget the joy as he proclaimed, "I have waited all day to share the good news with you. God heard your prayers and healed my wife. The cancer is gone. The test came back negative."

So often we do not really think about the form we display to others. Do we go out of our way to greet them with a smile? Like Torrance, do we wait expectantly for even just five minutes of interaction? This was one of the things I cherished about my great-grandmother. She was a woman who was very diligent in her greetings. Every time I went to see her, she would be waiting at the door. She would come out to greet me on the path up to the door and would always have a big hug waiting. I will never forget the feeling of her loving arms wrapping around me as she embraced me, holding me tight and pressing her cheek against mine. Oh, how I loved her. It felt so good to know that I was wanted and that someone in the world looked forward to spending time with me. We all need to feel that!

Do we make the most of our time with others? The Lord really grew this concept in me as I worked Hospice. In the type of Hospice I did, I had to travel from one home to the next and spend about an hour at a time engaging with people who I might not know at all. When I arrived, I had to greet, meet, and assess what their needs were. Some of the patients I met were not able to interact or speak. I remember one woman who was paralized and mute. Her breast cancer had advanced to the point that it was a big, infested wound in her chest. What a humbling experience. When she could not express her needs to me, I prayed, "Lord, what does this poor little woman need?" He responded, "Peace". I remember being taken aback. "How does one go about giving another peace". The Lord's response was not one I was ready for. He told me to sing to her. I'm a fighter and a wrestler. So many times, the Lord is clear and direct, but I have to question what He's saying. For me, the pressing issue was that I was not able to ask her if that was what she wanted. I had one choice in the matter. Would I choose to trust the Lord and His assessment and put into motion an act of obedience.

Second, the Bride's form displays the beauty the Lord has made unique to everyone. The Lord has made each of us so distinctly different. He has endowed us with such beautiful treasures to share with others. These treasures are spiritual gifts or spiritual disciplines the Lord gives so that we can complete the good works He has prepared for us to do. These treasures are meant to be shared, but most of the time, we are unwilling. We are hesitant. We are fearful to allow the beauty of our form to be displayed before the world. There was unwillingness at first in my heart. As I stood before that little woman who tossed and writhed in restless discomfort, I had no choice but to lay down all my hesitancy and unwillingness before the Lord. Taking a chair that was in the room, I pulled it up close beside her. With a smile I told her, "I hear that you love the Lord and that you used to be able to go to Church regularly. I'm sorry that your situation is such that you can't do that anymore. If it's ok with you, I'd like to sing and worship the Lord with you." She paused and stopped moving and just looked at me. A tear began to roll down her face. Placing my hand upon her arm, I began to pour out my heart before the Lord. She closed her eyes and took deep breaths. And I saw it…I saw the Lord's peace wash over her and then I felt it. I will never forget the peace of the Lord that entered into that room and washed over both of us. When I left that day, she was smiling and was laying still and looking comfortable.

As we look at our form, do we take the time to engage in harder discussions with others? Do we make time to know and understand one another's struggles and trials? Do we make time to know the thoughts upon their hearts? In Hospice, we usually are not allowed to accept anything from the patients. I will never forget Bob. He was such a lovely elderly man. He was the main caregiver for his beautiful wife of close to 50 years who was suffering from dementia. I remember my first visit. I came and Bob invited me into his home. He asked me to sit down at the table with him and he had cookies and coffee ready and set out on the table for me. I graciously attempted to decline his generous offer, but he would just not have it. The Hospice staff soon found out that this was what Bob needed to share his heart. He was from a Scandinavian family. The men in that culture would sit around the table with food and drinks and talk for hours. When the Hospice staff did not join Bob at the table, he felt as though he was not free to engage in conversation. In order to hear what was on his heart, we had to be willing to recline at the table with him. Do we take the time to understand what the needs of those the Lord has placed in our life are? Are we willing to invest in solutions if there is an issue in communication? Do we prepare a place for them to recline with us? Do we encourage them, build up, and restore the brokenness we encounter? I implore you, look for opportunities. Daily evaluate your form and make sure it is as lovely and as pleasing as it can be before the Lord and others.

The third aspect of the Bride's form deals with the glory or the light she carries. Matthew 25:1 says, "*At that time the kingdom of heaven will be like ten virgins who took their lamps and went out to meet the bridegroom.*" This is where our duties as the Bride cross over with those of being priests. The Lord commanded the priests that they were not to let the fire go out. This was for the altar of sacrifice before they entered the temple, and they were to keep the seven-fold menorah in the Holy Place continually burning. This represents the Bride's interactions with the Lord. If there is any sin in our lives, we are to bring it before Him on the altar before we enter in expecting to have an encounter with Him. But everything with the light within us does not just deal with surrender and sacrifice. How do we fill our light up so it can keep burning? We do this by being in the Presence of the Holy Spirit.

Isaiah 11 tells us that the Spirit of God is seven-fold. Each breath of His Spirit is defined by attributes of His glory: *"The Spirit of the LORD will rest on him—the Spirit of wisdom and of understanding, the Spirit of counsel and of might, the Spirit of the knowledge and fear of the LORD—and he will delight in the fear of the LORD."* These aspects of His glory are what He endows His Bride with. He clothes us in the beauty of His majesty so that when the world looks at us, all they see is a picture of His glory. How are we to keep our light burning? 2 Timothy 1:6 says, "*…fan into flame the gift of God, which is in you through the laying on of my hands.*" We are to lay hands on one another and ask and pray for the Holy Spirit to ignite these gifts of the Holy Spirit in one another.

The third aspect of the Bride's form is that she is found waiting for the coming of the Lord. I have become very fond of this spiritual discipline. Like many, there were so many years in my life that I did not understand what it truly meant to wait upon the Lord.

When I was in Seminary, I was taking a spiritual formation class and, in that class, we had to pick three spiritual disciplines to practice for the year. The professor encouraged us to pray and ask the Lord what disciplines He wanted us to work on. Waiting upon the Lord was one that He gave to me. As I began to look up Scripture about "waiting upon the Lord", I realized that the majority of the time the phrase used for "waiting upon the Lord" is used in context with "war" or "battle". This intrigued me. What does waiting have to do with war? I soon realized that the definition of waiting that I had grown up with was vastly different than what I found in Scripture.

I grew up understanding "waiting" to be more like passive meditation. One was to sit quietly in prayer and wait until they felt the presence of the Lord come. I can remember countless attempts of sitting in my quiet place just waiting to feel the presence of the Lord come, but the majority of the time I did not feel anything. This left me feeling very discouraged and I stopped pressing in due to the disappointment. This is not what the Hebrew meaning for "wait upon the Lord" is supposed to look like at all. The Hebrew word for "waiting" has the idea of "twisting together". As I sought the Lord for understanding to this concept, He gave me a vision that better explained it. I saw a child that had wrapped themselves around their father's leg and then as the father began to walk, the child was taken everywhere he went. This thought also brings to my mind the idea of dancing together. Waiting upon the Lord is not passive. It involves physical contact and a coming together. Notice in the vision, the child is the one that wrapped its little arms around its father's leg. So often we wait to feel a touch, but will we dare to just reach out and grab ahold of Him. That step of faith involves a willingness to allow the Spirit of God to move where He intends to go forth once we grab on, and a surrender to follow along with Him wherever He goes. Willingness and surrender are two aspects of the Bride's form that are vital to the full development of our faith. We cannot attain the full measure of Christ without them. As we move into the exploration of our identity as priests, we will see just how vital willingness and surrender are.

8

SACRED STEWARDSHIP BESTOWED UPON THE PRIESTS

"Then I passed by and saw you kicking about in your blood, and as you lay there in your blood I said to you, 'Live!' I made you grow like a plant from the field. You grew up and developed and became the most beautiful of jewels." Ezekiel 16:6-7

God is Spirit; therefore, it takes great faith for us to enter into that place of fellowship. In vision, I have seen it repeatedly, the tent on the front line of the battlefield. I hear the tent curtains flapping in the wind and I see the table the Lord has prepared. Who will enter into the tent of meeting? Who will prepare a meal before Him like Abraham did and then wait for His appearance and participation in the physical realm? We are making history just like our forefathers did. Our forefathers in the faith did not just record their history. They have given us the most beautiful gift by preserving a written record of their faith in action which resulted in a very real and tangible relationship with God. Isn't that what we all want…to have daily experiences with the Lord? What did the patriarchs of the Old Testament do in order to have those intimate encounters with God? It's all about entering into

His Presence. One can only enter in if they believe. Believing can be the hardest part if you struggle to hear, see, or feel in the spirit world. I have experienced the spirit world and heavenly dimensions through visions and dreams from a young age.

Just because you do not experience the spirit world does not mean that you cannot experience God. It was an act of faith that allowed Abraham, Moses, and the elders to attain an encounter with the Lord. Abraham's encounters with the Lord revolved around his day-to-day life. No matter where he was, he was always in conversation with the Lord. It was his active, earnest seeking that prompted the Lord to physically show up one day by the Tree of Mamre. When Abraham saw Him, he knew it was the Lord. It was not the first time he had experienced God, but this time the Lord showed up in a physical encounter. Abraham was so delighted that he hurried to get a meal prepared for the Lord so that they could sit together and fellowship. Many of us are not seasoned in long suffering. We set aside a small amount of time for the Lord and when we do not experience His presence, we leave disappointed. The continued disappointment grows until we give up and stop seeking. Here is what we need to change. If we want to experience the Lord, then, we must be willing to endure and just keep coming.

When I was seventeen, I was teaching Five Day Bible Clubs during the summer. I will never forget the little seven-year-old boy I met named Dakota. All summer, I had been teaching with another teen named Anne. We had gotten in a rhythm of sharing the club duties. Usually, I taught the Bible story and gave the salvation message and then would ask the children who wanted to know Jesus to come to the side. As I did this; Anne would continue the club with the rest of the children reading them a missionary story. But that day, Anne had not been able to attend with me. I was operating out of habit and before I knew it, I had finished the Bible story and was telling the children who raised their hands to come to the side room with me. Then I suddenly realized that I could not leave the others unattended and corrected myself telling them we would talk at the end. It was then that Dakota suddenly threw himself at my feet. Gripping the bottom of my skirt he began to shout, "No! I want to know Jesus now!" I tried to assure him that I would not leave without telling him about Jesus. But the more I argued, the louder he screamed, "NO! I WANT TO KNOW JESUS NOW!" I will never forget the passion in his voice. Oh, how I long to see such passion for the Lord among His people. Where are those who have that desire to seek and know the Lord?

Going back to Abraham's experience, I believe the Lord showed up with Abraham that day because He saw Abraham's heart. The Lord had given a promise to Abraham and watched through the years as Abraham passionately continued to believe against all odds that it would come to pass. But on that day in Mamre, the Lord Himself appeared to deliver the fulfillment of His word. Abraham prepared a meal before Him. They sat, ate, and fellowshipped. Notice that Abraham did not seek to know anything about the coming of the Lord's word. He simply enjoyed the fellowship. It was then that the Lord spoke. *"Then one of them (The Lord) said, "I will surely return to you about this time next year, and Sarah your wife will have a son." (Genesis 18:10)* After years of receiving no sign of anything even coming to pass, at the appointed time, the Lord released the word of fulfillment over Abraham. The Lord desires to be in an intimate relationship with us and searches out those who are seeking for deeper intimacy in His presence.

When the Lord called Moses and the elders to fellowship with Him, they had to climb up a mountain. Stop and think about that. How much time, effort, and work does it take to climb a mountain? "*Then the LORD said to Moses, 'Come up to the LORD, you and Aaron, Nadab and Abihu, and seventy of the elders of Israel.'" (Exodus 24:1)* In that place, they set a table and they prepared a meal. Scripture says that they talked and ate with God. This passage has fascinated me for years. A few years back, I had the opportunity to discuss it with a Rabbi. I had asked him to describe how he saw God. He admitted that he did not see God as a real person. He explained that many Jewish people see God not as a being, but as a derivative of all their collective thoughts. That is what they call "God consciousness". As he spoke, the Lord reminded me of this passage in Exodus 24 where twice in the passage it states that these men "saw" God. "*Moses and Aaron, Nadab and Abihu, and the seventy elders of Israel went up the mountain and saw the God of Israel. Under his feet was something like a pavement made of lapis lazuli, as bright blue as the sky. But God did not raise his hand against these leaders of the Israelites; they saw God, and they ate and drank.'" (Exodus 24: 9-11)*

I asked the Rabbi if God was only a collective thought in our minds, like he proposed, then, how could Moses and the elders have this experience? He explained that verses nine and eleven are very interesting. He said that in verse nine, it says the elders saw God with their spiritual eyes like in a vision. However, in verse eleven, the Hebrew word means that they literally saw God with their physical eyes. What a powerful thought! We serve a God who makes Himself known and seen to us. We do not need to strive to have these encounters. The Lord desires us to come into His Presence. Seeking does not mean striving to experience. It is just a matter of our being "willing" to make every effort to continually come into His presence for the purpose of relationship.

What I love most about the stories of the patriarchs, is that even though God is Spirit, their encounter of Him was very real within the physical realm. It can be hard to believe that God is real or that He is a living being. It is even harder for those who do not see, hear, or feel in the spiritual realm to believe that the Lord of all Creation will show up to fellowship with them and that they will be able to enter into that experience. Who can grasp all the ways that we can have physical encounters with the Lord? Yet, that is exactly what is preserved for us in Scripture. This is what became their testimonies. Do you preserve your intimate encounters with the Lord to share with others? Abraham, Moses, and the elders over Israel all walked, talked, and ate with God. Their actions were accounted to them as faith. I will never forget one of my most intimate encounters with the Lord. I was about two when I had my first very real physical encounter and then again at age five.

I remember my first time in Church at the age of two. That year, our house pipes froze and we had to move in with my father's relatives who were strong Christians who truly loved the Lord. They encouraged my mom to attend Church with them. I remember being the only child in the nursery with the nursery worker who was a little Mexican woman by the name of Lily. Every day, I praise the Lord for Lily. She was not like most nursery workers I've encountered later in life who like to water down the gospel. She believed that even as a small child that I could understand the truths from God's Word. The first time she read the Word of God to me, she sat me on her lap, opened the Bible across our laps and read to me from the Book of John. I will never forget as she read the story of John the Baptist saying, "Get ready, Jesus is coming." When I heard the

Word of God, my heart leaped, and I knew it was true. The Scripture verses she taught me, and the Bible songs became vital weapons in my little toolbox as I was brought into the System for training as the successor to my Proctor, the Queen Mother of Darkness.

As hard as it is to believe, all throughout my training, I encountered the Lord. The most memorable experience was around age five after I had refused to participate in my first ritual where I was supposed to take the life of an infant. We were in the sanctuary of a Catholic Church in Rockford, Illinois. In the center of the sanctuary was a square, dark, wood altar with engravings on all four sides. The engravings were images representing the demonic principalities Leviathan, Ashtoreth, Baal, and Molech. A dark wine-colored, red cloth was stretched across the top of the altar and hung down draping onto the floor on both sides. On the center lay an infant that had been given paralyzer, a golden chalice, and a dagger. This ceremony was not just a ritual killing. It also was to be a hidden marriage ceremony to the principalities.

There was a nine-year-old boy who was present with me. In this ritual we had been prepared to both cut our hands and drip our blood into the chalice, then we were to kill the infant together. He took the dagger first and fulfilled his part of the ritual, cutting his palm and then making a fist and holding it over the chalice to catch the blood. As he held his hand over the chalice cup, the dagger was handed to me. I remember being so angry at those around me and what they planned to do. I took the dagger, but instead of cutting my hand, I turned and chucked it at the face of my Proctor and as I did that, I swept my hand across the altar flinging the chalice with blood all over the floor. The silence in the room was deafening. It was as if those present were afraid to breathe for fear of the consequences that were surely on their way. The high priest was the first to move.

He grabbed me up and threw me over his shoulder like a sack of potatoes. Carrying me to the graveyard, he found an open grave and threw me down into the catacombs that connected to it. He put something over the top and left. I remember as I snuggled up against the dirt wall, I wondered if they would come back for me or if this would be my demise.

The Lord had other plans. I was not in the catacombs long when suddenly I saw a man walking towards me who looked like He was on fire, but without burning. As He got closer, I knew it was the Lord. I remember that He picked me up and took me in His arms. He held me close to His chest and carried me through the catacombs. I could see clearly as we walked because the light of His glory shone in the darkness.

The Lord took me to a little door and set me down before it. Then He said to me, "Ask of Me what you will?" I said to Him, "I want them all to come out." Then the Lord told me I would have to be brave and strong. He opened the little door and I stepped out back into the sanctuary where the sacrifice was supposed to occur. I came in behind the group of adults who were standing in a bunch arguing about what to do since their sacrifice had been ruined. I stood there quietly until someone suddenly noticed me. The high priest and my Proctor approached me. To this day, I think they honestly thought I had astral projected out of that catacomb. The high priest asked me, "How did you get here?" I replied, "Jesus let me out the door." He screamed, "What door?" I pointed to where it had been. But, he never believed me and hit me several times calling me a liar to my face. Even though he could not deny that I had somehow appeared there through a miracle, the priest did not want to believe that the Lord Himself had been a part of that miracle. That day, the Lord showed up in a very real and tangible way in my life. He worked a miracle that was greater than what I could have ever imagined. That miracle was the beginning of a much greater work that is being accomplished today as the Lord is fulfilling His great work to bring the captives out of the darkness.

We must seek to understand this great work of God because He is not just in the business of saving us from an eternal state of death. Everything that is currently happening is part of His bigger plan to bring about "a great salvation". John 6:29 says, "*Jesus answered, 'The work of God is this: to believe in the one He sent.'*" Who is this one? It is Jesus, the Son of God. The one whose blood was shed on the cross so that our sins could be forgiven. The purpose of belief is not just so that we may have salvation; it is a key that opens a much bigger door. John 11:40 says, *"Then Jesus said, 'Did I not tell you that if you believe, you will see the glory of God.'"* What is that bigger door that belief opens? Belief opens our eyes so that we may see His glory and experience His fellowship just as Abraham, Moses, and the elders did. It is through this fellowship that we enter into the place of ministering in His presence as priests.

What is the sacred stewardship we have as priests? I believe the first sacred stewardship we have as priests is to foster a discipline of fellowship with the Lord. You are the Bride of Christ, and you are a Kingdom of Priests. In my course "Dominion and Authority", I speak about the priestly duties we have been given. The most important thing to remember is that our duties are an act of worship and as such, the fulfillment of those duties must flow out of our relationship with the Lord. I will never forget the first time that I witnessed this in action. I was in prayer and suddenly found myself having a vision about the healing pools in heaven. The pools are a large, rectangular design with four tall, white, roman columns along each wall. They fill the entire room and look out toward the eastern gate. There is no fourth wall. The waters reach the eastern gate and flow out into a massive waterfall over the edge and out into the streams of living water that flow through heaven.

As I was watching in the vision, I saw the archangel Raphael standing upon the waters in the pool. He had two red worship flags in his hands that looked like twirling fire; he began to worship with them in dance before the Lord. I looked in awe as each moment was a prayer danced out before the Lord. As he worshiped, the waters in the pools were stirred up and began to sing new songs. The water was dispersed out of the temple in heaven and landed into the streams of living water below. Those streams contain water that is for the healing of the nations. What a beautiful sight! It was only after seeing this vision that I realized that even our angelic brethren join in worship and that all the Lord calls us to do comes out of the moments we spend in His presence offering up all we have as acts of worship. Therefore, with such beautiful acts of service set before us, should not every moment be embraced as one He has prepared for us? "*Therefore, I urge you brothers, by the mercies of God, to* offer *your* bodies *as a living sacrifice, holy and pleasing to God, your spiritual worship.*" *(Romans 12:1)*

Together, we and our angelic brethren are the Body of Christ. We are both physical and spiritual beings. We all have duties and jobs in the spiritual realm to perform. As such, it is important to define our priestly duties in both the physical and spiritual realm as we learn to live this newly transformed life we have in Christ. I do not believe that the spiritual duties Scripture describes for us are only to be practiced once we permanently leave this physical world. I believe our spiritual duties are to be applied now. Scripture tells us that the Kingdom of God is here now. *"'For the Kingdom of God is already among* you." ... *(Luke 17:21)* We have the Kingdom of God now. Do you believe that it is within you?

If you believe that the Kingdom of God is within you and that it is here now, then you know that the Father would not have us wait till we leave this world to put into practice the new life we possess. That is why He affords us every opportunity to learn how to live it out. Remember, everything here on earth is a replica of what is in Heaven. Tending to our physical and spiritual duties is part of our priestly role. It falls under the category of spiritual formation. Spiritual formation occurs in four main areas we use to grow our faith: 1) Being in the Word, 2) Prayer, 3) Worship and 4) Fellowship. Spiritual disciplines are the tools or applications we use to develop or advance our faith in these four main areas until we attain to the full measure of Christ.

Each of these areas have a physical and spiritual component to them. How do we begin to understand how to differentiate between the physical and spiritual components? The beginning of understanding these concepts starts with a base realization that you have a physical and spiritual body. Both are present here on earth with you but at the same time, your spiritual body is in Christ and present with Him in the spiritual realms. That means that you have access now to the spiritual realms of the Lord. Your bodies are not two separate bodies. They are one. What happens to one affects the other.

There are many Old Testament Books in the Bible that teach us about our priestly duties. But I believe the New Testament Book of Hebrews is the one that clarifies an understanding into who Christ is as the High Priest and therefore also what our duties as priests are to be. There is a sacred stewardship of God's house that is bestowed upon the priests. *"For this reason, we must pay closer attention to what we have heard, so that we do not drift away from it. For if the word spoken through angels proved unalterable, and every transgression and disobedience received a just penalty, how will we escape if we neglect so great a salvation? After it was at the first spoken through the Lord, it was confirmed to us by those who heard, God also testifying with them, both by signs and wonders and by miracles and by the gift of the Holy Spirit according to His own will." (Hebrews 2:1-4)*

What is the sacred calling that we have received that the author of Hebrews warns us not to neglect? It is the honor of being chosen to serve the Lord as a kingdom of priests. Not only has He chosen us for this duty, but He has appointed and anointed us to it. "*For He did not subject to angels the world to come, concerning which we are speaking. But one has testified somewhere saying, 'What is man, that You remember him? Or the son of man, that You are mindful of him? You have made Him for a little while lower than the angels; You have crowned him with glory and honor and have appointed him over the works of Your hands. You have put all things in subjection under his feet." (Hebrews 2: 5-8)* The Lord has put a crown upon our heads as a display that He has given to us authority in the Name of His Son over all things. We are not to neglect this sacred duty because it is a reflection of Jesus who has been appointed the Great High Priest; He who is faithful in all God's house.

Our authority only exists because it has been placed in the hands of our Lord and Savior Jesus Christ. We are asked to "consider" Jesus as the High Priest. *"Therefore, holy brethren, partakers of a heavenly calling, consider Jesus, the Apostle and High Priest of our confession;" (Hebrews 3:1)* This is the same concept used when Scripture says that Abraham "considered" God faithful, and it was accounted unto him as righteousness. What does that word "consider" mean? The word "consider" is a term used as one decides. It means to count or weigh all the possibilities.

For Abraham, this meant considering the Lord's words. The Lord had made Abraham two promises. First, that he would have an heir. Second, that he would have land and be a mighty nation. As he thought about these things, he was nearing the age of a hundred. So far, the Lord had not fulfilled His word to Abraham. As Abraham looked at himself and Sarah, he realized that it was nearing the time of their death. Instead of fearing the Lord would not fulfill His word, Abraham made a choice to believe in the Lord. This did not mean that he was only choosing to believe in thought. The word "considering" means that Abraham chose to live as though the Lord had already fulfilled His promises to him, even though they had not yet come to pass. Now let's look at what it means for us to "consider" Christ?

9

THE HORN OF OIL

"I counsel you to buy from Me gold refined by fire, so that you can become rich; and white clothes to wear, so that you can cover your shameful nakedness and salve to put on your eyes, so you can see." Revelation 3:18

When I first read Revelations 3:18, the only thing on my mind was, "How, Lord? How do I buy from You?" There are so many secret and hidden revelations to learn about in regard to the Kingdom of God. It is hard to make the shift from only seeing and thinking one dimensionally to multi-dimensionally. The Kingdom of heaven is not bound by one dimension, yet so many of us try to limit it to that. We can only find the answers we seek one way. We must enter into the Lord's presence through prayer and "considering". Let's start by considering Jesus, our High Priest. Who knows the Father better than He? *Lord, we ask that as we come right now into Your Presence that You will open our eyes that we may see and our ears so that we may hear all that You desire to reveal to us. In Jesus' Precious Name we ask.*

In Zechariah 3, we are shown a scene in heaven of "Joshua" the high priest standing before the angel of the Lord. I believe this scene describes Jesus going before the Father and the seven-fold Holy Spirit while another character emerges into the scene, "*...and Satan stood on His right side ready to accuse Him." (Zechariah 3:1)* This timeless battle between the Lord and the enemy of God is nothing new. Satan wanted to prevent, hinder, and stop the work of God then and he wants to do the same now. Any time the Lord's hand begins to move, the enemy goes before the Courts of heaven in an attempt to keep the priests from fulfilling their priestly duties. Why does he attack the priests? It is because the priests are the ones who hear the voice of God and receive the vision and the plans for the works He is about to release. As the Bride, we prepare the people for the works; as the priest, we prepare the land, God's house, and the Courts of heaven for the actual release of the great work the Lord is doing. This is a process.

As soon as a work begins, our adversary pulls us into the Courts of heaven to accuse us before the Lord and tell the Lord that we are unclean and, therefore, unfit to release the work of His hand. In Zechariah 3, we see Joshua the high priest representing the priesthood in his day, as well as the Priesthood of Yeshua that was to come. As he is pulled into the Courts, what does Satan accuse him of? Satan points out his filthy garments. The breakthrough we all need comes through this powerful passage. Do you understand that it is the Lord Himself who addresses Satan about the accusations being made. How does the Lord address Satan's accusations against His Kingdom of priests in that time and in the age to come? I can just hear His voice proceeding forth through the courts like a mighty torrent of water, "*The Lord rebuke you, Satan! The Lord, who has chosen Jerusalem, rebukes you! Is not this man a burning stick snatched from the fire?" (Zechariah 3:2)*

I believe there is a depth to the Word of God here that we will never truly understand in that phrase as He continues, "is not this man a burning stick snatched from the fire?" Jesus is the "begotten" Son. The only One in creation that is begotten. In the Hebrew language, the term "begotten" can represent a splinter being removed from a larger piece of wood. Our High Priest is the only begotten Son of God. He is that splinter that comes from God's own essence which is the Vine. What does it mean that He was like a stick snatched from the fire? He alone was able to bear the weight of God's wrath that burned against our sins without being consumed. Who can fathom the depth of God's all-consuming wrath? Yet, it is this wrath that breaks forth into His unfathomable love. What a beautiful display of the Father's love we see in this passage. His love is not just for His Son, it is for the One He has called to be the High Priest over His temple and His house. We see the Son standing before His presence in filthy clothes, stained, tainted, carrying the stench of one who has been in the fire. What does the Father say as He looks upon Him?

> *"Then He said to Joshua, 'See, I have taken away your sin, and I will put fine garments on you... Put a clean turban on his head.' So, they (the angels) put a clean turban on his head and clothed him, while the angel of the LORD stood by." (Zechariah 3:4-5)*

To enter into this priesthood, we must first open our eyes. What does the Lord command Joshua? He says, "See! See, I have already taken the filthy garments away." No longer was He standing in the Lord's presence in the filthy rags covered in the blood of the sin that He bore. No, the Supreme Judge of heaven and earth declares, "See, I have clothed you in new garments". There is nothing you can do on account of your sin or past. No amount of "works" will get you clean. Meaning there is nothing you can do to attain "cleanness". We must come to the place of surrender and acceptance. Your position in the priesthood is secured because of the work that Jesus Christ did on the cross by the power of His blood. It is sacred because it is His work alone. All you must do is open your arms to receive it and seek to understand what purposes He has called you to.

Our priestly calling comes with a great charge. After the Father clothed Jesus as the Great High Priest who sits at His right hand, He was empowered and received the priestly charge the Lord has spoken over the priesthood.

> *"The angel of the Lord gave this charge to Joshua: This is what the Lord Almighty says: 'If You will walk in obedience to Me and keep My requirements, then You will govern My house and have charge of My courts, and I will give You a place among these standing here. Listen High Priest Joshua, You and Your associates seated before You, who are men symbolic of things to come. I am going to bring my servant the Branch. See, the stone I have set in front of Joshua! There are seven eyes on one stone, and I will engrave an inscription on it.' Says the Lord Almighty, 'And I will remove the sin of this land in a single day! In that day, each of you will invite your neighbor to sit under your vine and fig tree,' declares the Lord." (Zechariah 3: 7-10)*

How are we to see? I believe it starts by understanding the thoughts the Lord has for us. One morning, I woke to the Lord saying, "I know the thoughts I have for you." He kept putting the emphasis on the words, "I know" as He spoke. I sensed that it was important to Him that I understood that He was very aware of the thoughts that He had towards me. As I listened, He showed me the thoughts that I had been entertaining and that those thoughts were not His thoughts. How powerful this revelation was. There is a spiritual discipline that goes hand in hand with entertaining thoughts. Scripture says we are to put on the mind of Christ. "*For who has understood the mind of the Lord so as to instruct him? But we have the mind of Christ." (1 Corinthians 2:16)* What does it mean that we have the mind of Christ? It means that we are able to hear His voice and we know His thoughts.

The Lord has shown me that the issue of entertaining thoughts is a huge issue among believers. We are not mindful of the thoughts we entertain about the Lord, ourselves, and others. This includes thoughts we have towards others and our perceived thoughts of what their thoughts are toward us. The biggest issue in the entertaining thoughts is pride and narcissism, also called self-focus. When we find thoughts coming, we must ask, "Whose thoughts am I entertaining?" We cannot assume to know another's thoughts nor assume they know ours. This is where the enemy begins to hold us captive in relationships to what I am calling the "entertaining cycle".

Assuming is a vicious cycle. Why? Because we never assume for the good, we only assume for the worst. Stop and think about the extent of this issue. We continue to entertain thoughts that only assume for the worst, while the Father says, *"I know the thoughts I have for you, thoughts for your good (peace), and not of evil, to give you a future and a hope." (Jeremiah 29:11)* When we assume it causes us to react with one of three emotional responses: 1) fear, 2) anger, and 3) hurt. These emotional responses leave us in a whirlwind of negative thoughts and cause us to: 1) withdraw our vulnerability, 2) withdraw our trust, and 3) withhold our agape love from one another.

I have to explain here that there are truly good people, but we must be cautious with whom we choose to build relationships, because there are evil people in this world. There are relationships where we will need to set up strong boundaries, to do so is wisdom. There are those we are to build relationships with, but the Lord does not expect us to build relationships with everyone.

So, what is the solution to the issue of the thoughts we entertain about God, ourselves, and others, and the thoughts that they have towards us? The solution starts by applying the spiritual discipline of putting on the mind of Christ. That means that we take out our Bibles and we ask the Lord to show us His thoughts. It may be helpful to write down the thoughts He shows you in a journal. After we know His thoughts, the second step is to assure yourself in those thoughts.

We can read it and know what the words say, but do we truly believe what the Lord says? The step of securing those thoughts and firming them up is very important. You may want to write or speak out the truths starting with, "*Lord, I believe what You have said of me…that I am…*".

This second step includes "chewing" or "thinking upon" what the Lord has said. What does He mean by it and what does He plan to do with what He has revealed to you about yourself? When we know the Lord's thoughts for us, we must apply them in our relationships. This is where vulnerability and building trust begin.

The third step in the process is coming to that place of vulnerability and trust and hearing the thoughts of others. There is only one way to hear. You have to be willing to ask and listen. This is the giving and receiving aspect in relationships. Many of us have learned to give well; however, we do not know how to receive well. I find there are two disciplines behind receiving: a) believing and b) considering. Putting these two spiritual disciplines into practice is how we break free from the negative "entertaining cycle". As we seek out the Lord's thoughts, we consider and choose to believe His thoughts and think on those. As we do that, there is no place for negative and unhealthy assumptions. This is an investment we are making in our relationships. If you want to form healthy communication in your relationships with one another, then you must hold fast to healthy investments in the way you think and perceive.

There is a beautiful example of the Lord's investment in us shown in Ezekiel 16:6-14. What aspect of His great work should we start with? First, He not only calls us to be priests serving in His house and in His Courts. He calls us to "live". *"...Then I passed by and saw you kicking about in your blood, and as you lay there in your blood I said to you, 'Live!'"* Secondly, He tends to us. He raises us up paying close attention to every detail of our lives so that we have the best He can offer us, "*I made you grow like a plant of the field. You grew up and developed and became the most beautiful of jewels. Your breasts were formed, and your hair grew, you who were naked and bare."*

Thirdly, His love for us grows and He adorns us to reign and rule by His side, "'*Later I passed by, and when I looked at you and saw that you were old enough for love, I spread the corner of my garment over you and covered your nakedness. I gave you My solemn oath and entered into a covenant with you,' declares the Sovereign LORD, 'and you became mine.' I bathed you with water and washed the blood from you and put ointments on you. I clothed you with an embroidered dress and put leather sandals on you. I dressed you in fine linen and covered you with costly garments. I adorned you with jewelry: I put bracelets on your arms and a necklace around your neck, and I put a ring on your nose, earrings on your ears and a beautiful crown on your head. So, you were adorned with gold and silver; your clothes were of fine linen and costly fabric and embroidered cloth. Your food was fine flour, honey and olive oil. You became very beautiful and rose to be a queen. And your fame spread among the nations on account of your beauty, because the splendor I had given you made your beauty perfect,' declares the Sovereign LORD."*

As we look at Jesus, we see that He is the perfect High Priest appointed in the order of Melchizedek; He who lives forever. "Appointed" means to be called by God into that position. Hebrews 5:5-6 tells us that Jesus received His calling from God at His baptism where the Father spoke out of heaven, "*You are my beloved Son; in You I am well pleased.*" Also, the Father says of Him, "You are a priest forever in the order of Melchizedek." What is needed to be appointed? Scripture says, "*Every high priest is appointed on behalf of men in things pertaining to God, in order of offer both gifts and sacrifices for sin." (Hebrews 5:1)* Going back to Ezekiel 16, we see there was something greater that was poured out over the land. The investment the Lord makes in us is like the oil from a ram's horn being poured out. It is an oil of life and once it is poured out upon us, we are commissioned to pour what we have received out upon others. We are to invest in His Kingdom by investing in one another. What is the currency of this investment? It is the oil of "life". Get ready, we are learning how to tend, adorn, and display one another's beauty before the nations.

10

THE VOICE OF THE GROOM AMONG THE CHAMBERS

"Yet their voice [in quiet evidence] has gone out through all the earth, Their words to the end of the world. In them and in the heavens, He has made a tent for the sun, which is as a bridegroom coming out of his chamber; It rejoices as a strong man to run his course." Psalm 19:4-6

Jesus alone is our Great High Priest. Have you ever stopped to wonder what His House and Courts look like? We are called to partake within this sacred priesthood which means that He gives us access to enter into His house and His courts. We are told all authority belongs to Him in the heavens and the earth.

Some churches teach that men are on equal ground with Jesus because they do not teach the truth about Him. He is the Word who became flesh. The term "begotten" is vital to understanding His authority. The Son of God is the only one in all creation who is begotten. It means to "proceed forth from God's own essence." We are created or made in His image, but we are not a piece of His essence, coming from His glory. This is what makes Jesus fully human (God come in the flesh) and fully God. All created things were a breath spoken out of a manifestation of His glory. *"Therefore, holy brethren, partakers of a heavenly calling, consider Jesus, the Apostle and High Priest of our confession." (Hebrews 3:1)* How can we neglect such a great salvation? The priest's ministry before the Lord is to make all things subject under His feet.

Let's consider what this ministry of subjection entails and how it looks in Jesus' role as High Priest. There are seven main areas where Jesus ministers before the Lord and to us in His priestly capacity:

1) Cleansing sacrifice
2) Offering of prayers
3) Washing by the water of the Word
4) Supplications and petitions
5) Obedience through suffering
6) Releasing the word of righteousness-the meat of God's Word
7) Trained to discern good from evil.

We are made in the image of God. Our priestly role is a reflection of our Lord and Savior. As He is the Great High Priest, so He has called us to walk after Him doing as He does. "*For I am the LORD your God; consecrate yourselves, therefore, and be* holy, *because I* am holy..." *(1 Peter 1:16)* Imagine the scene in heaven of the four living creatures bowing down before the throne. As they cry out about His holiness and worthiness, you see Him; the Lamb standing before the throne. Such humbleness! Such majesty; His eyes blazing like fire. And He summons you to come into His Presence. As you come, He speaks to you. "I have made you to be a Kingdom of priests in the order of Melchizedek forever. Follow Me!"

I get chills when I think about the power of His blood that purchased us to be a Kingdom of priests. This calling is not something you need to achieve. It has already been prepared for you. He has prepared a place for you as a priest in His courts. Daily He calls you to come and assures your heart, "*But you are a chosen people, a royal priesthood, a holy nation, God's special possession, that you may declare the praises of Him who called you out of darkness into His wonderful light." (1 Peter 2:9)* Again, the Word of God says, "*And they sang a new song, saying: 'You are worthy to take the scroll and to open its seals, because You were slain, and with Your blood you purchased for God persons from every tribe and language and people and nation." (Revelations 5:9)*

Who can fathom what the role of a priest in the house of God entails? In the Old Testament, we see that the priesthood was a sacred duty and entering into the house of the Lord only took place at certain times. There was such a fear and reverence for the Lord that the priests would wear bells on the bottom hem of their garments and ropes around their foot so they could be pulled out of the temple in case the Lord struck them dead when they entered into the place where He was. Beloved, we have no need to fear. The Lord Himself has secured the way for us giving us full access to His presence and removing the veil between the Holy and Most Holy place so that we can enter into His presence with boldness. That is a word we need to hear more often among the people of God. We need more priests that boldly enter in.

As priests, who is our service to? *"He was faithful to the one who appointed Him, just as Moses was faithful in all God's house." (Hebrews 3:2)* We are in service to Him who appointed us. We are to be faithful in all God's house just as Moses was appointed to be faithful in all God's house. Verses 2-6 speak to how we are to be faithful in God's house. Our faithfulness is to be in the area of testifying to "these things". What things? About what Christ as the High Priest has accomplished and about our priestly duties to the Lord. What does this testimony we are to give look like? Well, we can take the easy way out. We can look up Scriptures about the Lord being our High Priest and we can share those Scriptures with others. This way is not the most fulfilling, although it is good and gets the job done. We are called to something much more costly. I say costly because it requires a price in order to be obtained. We are called to have a personal relationship with the Lord that we can share with others. We are the priests who are not just called to get the job done, we are called to get the job done and to live to tell about it. We are called to be most excellent! That means that we must go above and beyond. Men are not drawn to Christ just by hearing what the Word of God says about Him. They are drawn when they share the Word in light of their experiences of Him. The hearts seeking Him want an experience of God. Will you answer that call and give it to them? In order to give them an experience, you must be willing to testify to your experience of Him.

I will never forget one of the first times I experienced the Lord. I was at a large Church for a conference. At the end, the pastor gave an altar call and encouraged us to come to the front before the Lord. I was one who took every opportunity to present myself before Him. I went forward, kneeling down, putting my face on my hands on the ground. I remember I had seen two elder men going around laying hands on people and praying over them.

As I remained bowing, I sensed one of the men approach me and felt him put his hand on top my head. Instead of praying in English, I heard him praying in a tongue I could not distinguish. It was so beautiful and melodic. I remember thinking that it sounded like a sweet poetic song. As he continued to pray in this way, I sensed he knelt down in front of me while keeping his hand on my head. Then, he too got down on his knees. Bowing down, he pressed his head against the top of mine. I was so moved by his actions that I began to cry. In that moment of sweetness, curiosity got the better of me and I could not help but look up to see which of the two elderly men it was. As I lifted my head, I was shocked to see that no one was there. Immediately, the Spirit of the Lord spoke His word over me, "*In the same way, the Spirit helps us in our weakness. We do not know what we ought to pray for, but the Spirit himself intercedes for us through wordless groans. And he who searches our hearts knows the mind of the Spirit, because the Spirit intercedes for God's people in accordance with the will of God." (Romans 8:26-27)*

That day, the Lord touched me in a physical and tangible way that I will never forget. He came down to where I was and I heard Him praying over me offering up intercessions for me. As priests, we are called to testify to our personal experiences with the Lord. Our experiences can be good or bad. If we are entering in to spend quality time with the Lord, our experiences with Him will be good. If we make no time or use our time to cater to our fleshly desires, our experience of the Lord will be non-existent. You must choose. All are called to the sacred priesthood but not all will be faithful to steward that position well. What kind of priest do you choose to be before the Lord?

The Book of 1 Samuel shows us two types of priests. First, you have the priestly house of Eli. Scripture tells us that Eli's two sons, Hophni and Phinehas, were not faithful in the Lord's house. At the core, their hearts were rotten. What were their sins? These two men were called to enter into the Lord's presence with a heart of worshipful service. Yet, instead, when they offered sacrifices on the altar, instead of appropriating the portions of meat as the Lord had instructed, they kept back the best portions of meat for themselves. We are also told that they engaged in sexual sins with women who served in the house of God. I can almost hear the Lord crying out, "Who dares to trample before My presence with such sins?" WHO??? Their sin caused the Lord's anger to burn against them resulting in His harsh judgment against the house of Eli. *"This shall be the sign to you, that shall come on your two sons, on Hophni and Phinehas: in one day they shall both die." (1 Samuel 2:34)* The house of Eli was given opportunity to leave a legacy that would raise up generations that would honor God. They made a choice to follow after the pleasures of the flesh instead of honoring God. Because no obedience was found in their hearts, the Lord brought the house of Eli to an end.

I am confident that you will choose well. That you will not take this sacred calling lightly. We are not created in the order of Eli's house. God has given us a second option. We have a Great High Priest, Jesus Christ, who was faithful in all God's house. We were chosen to partake in His legacy. This generation has been called to not only serve before the Lord. We are those who reign with Him, governing, and administering His just and righteous judgements. How do we get these experiences? There is only one way to experience the Lord. You must make time for that experience. This time that we set aside is our spiritual act of service. Our service time is made up of duties. What do these duties consist of? The priests of old were called to enter into His presence. So, into the tabernacle of fellowship with the Lord we must go.

11

TABERNACLE OF FELLOWSHIP

"With great power the apostles continued to testify to the resurrection of the Lord Jesus. And God's grace was so powerfully at work in them all." Acts 4:33

This is no longer your everyday type of faith. The things you once learned or thought you knew; you must now leave behind. Place them in the grave with Jesus Christ and do not look back, because they are dead and gone. He has made you new. You have abundant life and He will give to you the full measure of Christ. There is no more holding back. Today is the day of salvation. Today is the day we enter into the heavenly house of the Living God to do His will.

How do we ENTER in?

By FAITH we believe!

Who will seek out the Kingdom of heaven? Who will search for the city of the Living God? As you enter towards the city, the outskirts of heaven are a series of pasturelands. These are fields that are part of the inheritance of the sons of God. At the entrance of the city stands a gate. The gate represents the One we must enter through. Our Lord and Savior Jesus Christ. He is the true Shepherd. All who want to enter into the Kingdom of heaven can only do so through Him. Why? Because He is the gate and He and the Father are One. Those who wish to come into the Presence of the Lord must believe that Jesus, the Father, and the seven-fold Holy Spirit are One. It is the only way. Do you believe this? Then enter in.

In John 10:1, Jesus says, *"Very truly I tell you Pharisees, anyone who does not enter the sheep pen by the gate, but climbs in by some other way, is a thief and a robber."* Why is going through Jesus the only way? Jesus does not say this because there is only one entrance into heaven. If that were true, He would not have said what he says in John 10:1. We see that there are other entrances over the wall around the city of God. Those who are not true shepherds after the Lord's heart, like the Pharisees, attempt to enter into the Kingdom of God by alternative means. This accusation that Jesus makes against the Pharisees is actually quite serious. Jesus is not just making a statement here. He is calling out the Pharisees out in regards to their sin of rejecting God and the Messiah He had sent and confronting the heart of the issue. What is the issue? The issue is that in their pride they seek to set themselves or others upon the heavenly throne as God. This is the same sin Satan fell prey to: pride. All throughout the Scriptures we see the Lord confronting Israel in their relationship with Him. What does He say?

> *"And the LORD said to Moses, 'Go, get down! For your people whom you brought out of the land of Egypt have corrupted themselves. They have turned aside quickly out of the way which I commanded them. They have made themselves a molded calf, and worshiped it and sacrificed to it, and said, "This is your god, O Israel, that brought you out of the land of Egypt!" And the LORD said to Moses, 'I have*

seen this people, and indeed it is a stiff-necked people! Now therefore, let Me alone, that My wrath may burn hot against them and I may consume them. And I will make of you a great nation.'" (Exodus 32:7-10)

Why did the Lord's anger burn so much against Israel? His anger against them goes back to His relationship with Abraham. The Lord visited Abraham at the trees of Mamre.

"One hot summer afternoon while Abraham was sitting by the entrance to his tent near the sacred trees of Mamre, the LORD appeared to him. Abraham looked up and saw three men standing nearby. He quickly ran to meet them, bowed with his face to the ground, and said, 'Please come to my home where I can serve you. I'll have some water brought, so you can wash your feet, then you can rest under a tree. Let me get you some food to give you strength before you leave. I would be honored to serve you.' 'Thank you very much,' they answered. 'We accept your offer.' Abraham went quickly to his tent and said to Sarah, 'Hurry! Get a large sack of flour and make some bread.' After saying this, he rushed off to his herd of cattle and picked out one of the best calves, which his servant quickly prepared. He then served his guests some yogurt and milk together with the meat. While they were eating, he stood near them under the tree, and they asked, 'Where's your wife Sarah?'" (Genesis 18: 1-10)

In that place, as Abraham prepared a meal before Him, the Lord released to Abraham the word of the coming fulfillment of His promise to Him. Abraham had waited almost to the point of death for God's word to be fulfilled to him. When all hope was just about gone, the Lord Himself came to deliver the release so that the promises could begin to unfold and come to completion. What was that spoken word of release? *"By this time next year, Sarah your wife will give birth to a child." (Genesis 18:10)*

The ability to fellowship with the Lord is a sacred moment. Is there any other God, who takes the time to fellowship, one who sits, eats, walks, and communes with those who will tarry? We have a God who desires to bestow good gifts upon us and freely meet all of our needs. He has prepared "a future and a hope for us". He has formed and prepared days and good works for us in advance. He wants to distribute these things but if we do not show up to fellowship, how can He do so? Those who are thieves and come to steal try to enter into heaven another way and take the goodness of God for themselves without having a relationship. That is why Jesus says, *"I am the door, through me if anyone may come in, he shall be saved, and he shall come in, and go out, and find pasture." (John 10:9)* Again, *"Jesus saith to him, 'I am the way, and the truth, and the life, no one comes unto the Father, if not through me;" (John 14:6)*

With such riches so lavishly given to us, why would anyone ever want to enter another way. Those that steal only can get so much. The wealth of the Kingdom of heaven has width, height, depth, and breath to it. And you can only get that full measure from the Living God. That is why His word says in Matthew 16:19 "*And this Rock will be the bed rock foundation on which I will build my Ekklysia, my legislative assembly, and the power of death will not be able to overpower it. I will give you the keys to the Kingdom to forbid on earth what is forbidden in heaven and to release on earth what is released in heaven."*

"His Kingdom is not a matter of talk, but rather a matter of power." (1 Corinthians 4:20)

What does "entering in" look like in practicality? It is as simple as praying and asking. You can pray along with me right now. Remember that His word says we must enter by faith and that we must believe. Does that mean that when we pray, we are going to see visions of heaven and our spiritual hearing and awareness will immediately be opened up? No, it does not mean that. The Word says, "*Jesus said to* him, *'Because you have* seen *Me, do you now* believe*?* Blessed *are they who* did not see *Me and* yet *believe.'" (John 20:29)* To enter in by faith means that we believe even if we do not see. And we keep coming into His Presence trusting that He has every intention of meeting with us. So let us pray.

Heavenly Father, we come boldly to the throne of grace. We glorify and lift up Your Name above every other Name that is in heaven and upon the earth. Who is like you? You alone are worthy of all praise, all honor, and all glory. You are greatly praised because You inhabit the praises of Your people. We trust that You are here with us because You have said that wherever two or more of us are gathered in Your Name that here You are in the midst of us. Lord, I have never been in Your house or Your courts before. In faith, I choose to trust that You will walk me through this process and that You will teach me how to operate in Your house and courts. I ask that You will counsel and instruct me. I want to know and understand the good works that You have prepared in advance for me. I ask that You will reveal them to me. I ask this in the precious Name of Jesus.

Now trust that You are there in His Presence. If you have any visions or any revelations from the Lord, write them down. I keep an account of everything because just when I think I have experienced it all the Lord will take me to new heights of depths. I entered into one of these deeper seasons a few months back. A year prior to this time, a friend had sent me a ram's horn, also called a shofar. I had seen shofars used before as an instrument that is blown like a trumpet. I practiced with mine and watched several videos, but all to no avail. One night the Lord woke me and said, "Your shofar is not a war shofar" (meaning it is not to be blown). He continued, "Your shofar is for anointing and priestly duties." I did not know what He meant since I had never seen it used that way before, but I remembered what the Lord had first told me about revelations, that if I did not understand, I was to ask Him for further revelation in the matter.

As I asked, the Lord instructed me to set my shofar on a table. He said every day I was to take some of the anointing oil that I had and put a drop of the oil into the shofar. At the same time, I was to remove a drop onto my finger and anoint myself with it. I didn't know yet what He was teaching me or the further purposes in it, but I knew He was going to show me. So, I dedicated myself to following His instructions every day. After about two weeks, I had the first revelation in a series of what I call "revelation puzzles". I call them that because I receive only a piece and not the full revelation at one time.

The first piece I received while visiting with family. On my way home from the visit, I was driving through a place where I had experienced childhood abuse. I made a stop in the area to get gas, eat, and stretch for a few minutes. There was a little market that I entered. Right as I went in the door, I saw three little, glass bottles with cork tops on them. The Lord told me to buy one of the glass bottles. I did so in obedience and headed out to the car. As I walked along the side of the grass in the parking lot, the Lord drew my attention to a plot of dirt and told me to anoint it and then scoop up some and put it into the bottle. I put the cork topper back on the top of the bottle and continued on my journey home.

The next morning, I checked my messages and realized a friend had sent me a video by Dr. Francis Myles called, "Speak to the Earth". As I listened, Francis directed those listening to restore a right relationship between themselves and the earth. He explained that in Genesis, the Lord created the earth to "bear forth fruit" on our behalf. He further explained that the earth is one of two witnesses in the Courts of heaven for us and because of bloodshed and sin the earth, the earth is in a position where it must testify to the evil and wickedness we do, and therefore, the land is under a curse and only releases curses back to us. In order to return to the right relationship which the Lord designed we need to confess and repent of our sin against God's creation and ask for forgiveness. Then because of our renewed right standing, we are to command the earth to return to the Lord's original design and command that it bear fruit for our good. I encourage you to get the book or watch his videos on this concept. This Biblical teaching in its fullness is very powerful. I believe that as more and more of the sons of God put it into motion that we are going to see the miracles, signs, and wonders released that we have been waiting for.

After hearing this teaching, the Lord instructed me to take the dirt I had put into the bottle like Francis suggested and to place it into my hand. After confession and repentance before the Lord, I stood outside and said, "Earth, I command you to bear forth on behalf of the sons of God according to the right relationship the Lord has reinstated between us. I ask for the release of the fruit and blessings that the Lord has prepared for me. I command you to bear forth life." I poured a little of the dirt on the ground and went back in the house, setting the bottle next to the ram's horn I had on the table.

The next few days, I got up and tended to the oil in the shofar. On the third day, the first miracle was released. I went to anoint my head with oil and the bottle of dirt caught my eye. As I lifted it up to have a closer look, I saw that the bottle was full of bright, green grass. I thanked the Lord and headed to my office to work on my writings. I sat down to write and the moment I opened up my Bible, the Lord began to show me a massive vision about His establishment of time, days, seasons, and the ordering of time according to our earthly and heavenly duties. I understood that this was part of the act of tending His house and that it connected to the cycle calendar of fruit and the Solomonic symbols of how the universe works and operates that I shared in session two of my Course, "Foundations of Kingdom Living".

The vision took place in the temple of God. I found myself standing in the holy place facing the doorway between the holy place and the Most Holy place. As I looked at the doorway, the veil that separated the two rooms hung there and was split in two. To the side of the door, I saw a thin, wood dowel. I took the dowel and starting at the bottom of the veil, I rolled both split pieces up and placed the rolled veil on a peg that was at the top of the doorway so that the glory of the Lord could proceed out. As I looked, I noticed I had seen that peg before and knew its name. It is called, "Be anxious for nothing". Five years prior to this time, I found myself in a position with a shoulder that continued to receive injury through multiple tears. I ended up having to have three surgeries. The third day after the second surgery, I had a bad reaction to the anesthetics and ended up in the hospital because I could not stop vomiting. One of my dear friends offered to keep me company for a while and read Scripture to me. I remember that he asked me what book I wanted him to read from and I asked for the book of Romans. He started to read and the last thing that came through my mind before I passed out was a vision that made me a little anxious. I saw myself laying in a hammock with a lone peg securing it to the side of a vast cliff. All I could see outside of the hammock was a bright array of clouds. The Lord sensed my anxiety and turned my eyes towards the peg. As I looked, He said, "The peg is secure. It has a name. It is called, 'Be anxious for nothing.'" So, when I saw the same peg in my vision in the holy place, I knew the Lord was giving me further revelation about the peg. As I stood and looked at the peg, I saw the door frame between the rooms change from a rectangular, wood frame to one of solid, heavy rock. At the time, I did not know why the Lord had caused the door to change to rock so I asked for further revelation.

The Lord showed me that this vision was about the release of Kingdom fruits according to the time and seasons. I saw the temple articles and how they were positioned in such a way that they reminded me of the numbers representing hours on a clock. I saw that each hour had fruit that needed tending. Each hour had preparation work that had to be finished in order to accomplish the good works that the Lord had prepared for the hours that followed. A piece of this work included rest. If the preparation work was incomplete, the fruit in the next hour could not be born and caused delays that bore dead fruits. I understood that this clock I saw in the vision represented fruits and was an important piece to understanding the fulness of the massive revelation the Lord was unfolding. I just did not know yet what to expect next.

12

ONE THING I HAVE ASKED

"One thing have I asked of the Lord, that will I seek after: that I may dwell in the house of the Lord all the days of my life, to gaze upon the beauty of the Lord and to inquire in his temple." Psalm 27:4

Blessed are those who come into the house of the Lord to fellowship with Him. Did you ever stop to think about the Beatitudes? They are rights that give us access into the Kingdom of God that are lovingly spoken over us by our Great High Priest, Jesus Christ.

> *"Blessed are the poor in spirit, for theirs is the kingdom of heaven.*
>
> *Blessed are those who mourn, for they will be comforted.*
>
> *Blessed are the meek, for they will inherit the earth.*
>
> *Blessed are those who hunger and thirst for righteousness, for they will be filled.*
>
> *Blessed are the merciful, for they will be shown mercy.*

Blessed are the pure in heart, for they will see God.

Blessed are the peacemakers, for they will be called children of God.

Blessed are those who are persecuted because of righteousness, for theirs is the kingdom of heaven.

Blessed are you when people insult you, persecute you and falsely say all kinds of evil against you because of Me.

Rejoice and be glad, because great is your reward in heaven, for in the same way they persecuted the prophets who were before you." (Matthew 5:3-12)

So where is this place where we can enter into the presence of God and are blessed? In the Old Testament we see several structures or places where the presence of the Lord was seen where Israel could enter in to worship Him. The first was the tabernacle. The second was the temple that Solomon built. The Tabernacle was a tent like structure that the Lord commanded Moses to construct. It was a movable house of worship modeled as an exact replica of the Temple in heaven. Because the Tabernacle was a tent, Israel was able to move with it as they followed the Lord in the wilderness for forty years. The Temple also was modeled off the heavenly Temple but it was a permanent building constructed in Israel. Both the Tabernacle and the Temple were sectioned off into four parts:

1) the Outer courts which had the altar of sacrifice,

2) the Inner Courts which had the water basin for cleansing,

3) the Holy Place where you would find the menorah, the twelve bread cakes, the utensils, and the veil, and

4) the Most Holy Place contained the Ark of the Covenant which held a jar of manna, the stone slab with the Ten Commandments written on it, and Aaron's staff that had budded.

We are called to enter into the presence of the Lord. Do you know what that means or how that is to be accomplished? "Entering in" is a sacred term. In the Old Testament, only the High Priest was allowed to enter into the Holy of Holies, the most intimate place of fellowship with God, and that was only once a year. But now, because Jesus paid the price for us to be a Kingdom of Priests, the veil that separated man from God is torn. Because the veil is torn, we can enter in any time.

"Through him we have the access -- we both -- in one Spirit unto the Father." (Ephesians 2:18)

"In whom we have the freedom and the access in confidence through the faith of Him," (Ephesians 3:12)

The access has been granted. All that is needed is a relationship with Jesus. He is the gate that we are to enter through. Because of His work on the cross, we are able to enter boldly into His presence because Jesus has made us righteous through the forgiveness of our sins. Dealing with sin is really where our priestly duties begin. Let's take a moment to look at the design of the temple of God. Remember, everything on earth is a replica of what is in heaven. That means your very own body is an image of what is in heaven. Your body represents the outer court, the inner court, the Most Holy Place, and the Holy of Holies. Your body is the place where the Lord dwells and where we can enter into the most sacred place of intimacy with the Living God.

> *"Let us therefore come boldly to the throne of grace, that we may obtain mercy and find grace to help in time of need." (Hebrews 4:16)*

> *"Therefore, brethren, since we have confidence to enter the holy place by the blood of Jesus, by a new and living way which He inaugurated for us through the veil, that is, His flesh, and since we have a great priest over the house of God." (Hebrews 10:19)*

Here we must pause and also give a warning. The Lord has created a special place for us to experience intimacy with Him. We have freedom to enter in at any time. However, with that freedom, there is a caution. Why does Hebrews chapters three and four speak so harshly about not entering in? Those who enter His presence; those who receive access must BELIEVE! This is where we must learn to live using our spiritual senses, as well as our physical senses. When you enter, you are accessing a spiritual realm of power. It is not defined or bound by physical laws or boundaries. It is more than we could hope, dream, or imagine. Who can fathom the place He has prepared for those who believe? *"However, as it is written: "What no eye has seen, what no ear has heard, and what no human mind has conceived" — the things God has prepared for those who love him." (1 Corinthians 2:9)*

Yet, at the same time, the Lord knows our hearts. Israel was a nation whose hearts were far from the Lord. Even when He provided everything for them, they grumbled and complained. They did not want intimacy with God. Rather, they wanted to live their own lives seeking self, pleasure, and money, and they expected God to allow them to do so. Their hearts were so far from God that they could not even rest in His Presence for one night. That is why in Hebrews chapters three and four we are told that the Lord's anger burned against them and He swore that they would not enter into His rest. So, the warning is this: be diligent to contend for your faith and your time with God. Don't get so busy or distracted that you do not make time. At this time, you are free to enter into His presence at any time. Don't take advantage of or misuse that Kingdom right because it will not be there forever. There comes a day when the Lord shuts the door.

Hebrews 3:11 commands us to "hold fast to our confession". What is our confession? I believe Jesus is the Son of God who died to cleanse me from my sin and raise me to new life. I now have the authority to enter as a priest into the Lord's presence and to minister before Him.

John 18: 37-38 *"The priests said to Him (Jesus), 'Art thou the king then?' Jesus answered, 'You say that I am a king. To this end I was born, and for this cause came I into the world, that I should bear witness to the truth. Every one that is of the truth hears my voice."*

13

THE PRIEST KNOWS THE INTIMATE CHAMBERS

"I clothed you with an embroidered dress and put sandals of fine leather on you. I dressed you in fine linen and covered you with costly garments." Ezekiel 16:10

How seriously does the Lord take His love? That is a question I hope to not only answer, but pray by the end of this chapter you will know that love which has no height, no width, no breadth, and no depth. What the Lord has put on my heart to share in these matters, I refer to as the Bride theology or Chambers of the Heart theology. This theology is based off a concept that the imagery of the Temple of God and its layout is an image of the stages of intimacy between the Lord and His Bride. In this theology, the concept of the chambers of the Temple breaks down by showing how we are to relate to the Lord in our relationship through different levels of intimacy. The Lord has shown me throughout the years that this imagery of the chambers is multi-layered and experienced, based on how much time we spend with Him. To gain a deeper understanding, one must be willing to devote themselves to time in the Lord's presence. How much time are you willing to commit to daily?

The release of the miracle I am about to share took place in two stages and could only be released through obedience. First, one night in prayer, the Lord told me to start putting oils in my bath every day. The oils He instructed me to add were called Esther oil and the Lion of Judah Oil. In obedience, I began to bathe in the oils nightly. The Lord also instructed me to start removing a drop of oil from the horn every morning and anointing myself with it and then pouring a drop of oil back in it. I was very curious as to why He was instructing me to do this. I could feel a release and breakthrough was around the corner but was left waiting in hopeful expectation.

The second part of this miracle began a year prior to this directive. I shared in an earlier chapter how around Fall time; a special friend surprised me with a shofar. I had seen shofars and had seen individuals sound them by blowing them like a trumpet. But I was clueless as to how to be faithful with this gift. I began to research in an attempt to learn how to play it. I spent time trying to figure out how to make it sound, but to be honest, playing it was a struggle. As I continued my studies, the Lord began to draw me into visions of the different chambers.

Visions From The Lord

(I shared this story prior, but I'd like to highlight further revelations from it).

One night, the Lord spoke to me, "It is not a war shofar that is to be sounded. Your shofar is a horn for oil. It is for healing." His words stirred my curiosity, and I began to ask Him to show me what

He meant. The release of His meaning came through a series of revelations.

The first revelation was simply a matter of random events. I have pictures of the Bride of Christ designed by my dear friend James Nesbit upon my piano in my living room. One of the pictures shows a long chambered hallway with big archways that leads to a single doorway. Standing at the end of the long hallway is a Bride beautifully adorned and walking toward the door. I had given a key to someone taking care of my house while I was gone, only to return and find the key strategically placed standing upright on the piano against that picture and pointing to the Bride and the door. It was almost as if the Lord was trying to point out that He was giving me the keys to the inner chambers.

The second revelation began while I was away from home. I had driven through a place where I experienced trauma as a child. I stopped at an old antique barn and as I walked in the door, I saw three small glass jars with cork stoppers. The Lord directed me to purchase the three bottles. As I went outside, I had been anointing the land with oil on my shoes, but the Lord directed me to take out the bottle of oil and to pour the oil upon the land. After following His directions, the Lord told me to take one of the bottles and put some of the land with the oil on it into the bottle. So, I scooped up a handful of dirt and put the cork lid back on it.

When I got home, I put the bottle of earth beside the shofar on the shelf. That evening, a friend called me to share a video he had found. The video was by Francis Myles, a pastor out of Africa. In the video, Francis Myles spoke about the original design of the Lord in the relationship between mankind and the land. He said that sin had caused a separation in that relationship and that the Lord desired a "right relationship" to be re-established. He broke down different verses that spoke to the restored original design which included our realm of responsibility as priests and sons of God. He showed how speaking to the earth was within the capacity of that realm of duties and encouraged those listening to express their authority by commanding the earth to "bring forth" according to the Lord's command in the book of Genesis. As I got to the end of the video, the Lord prompted me to pray along with Francis Myles and to command the earth to "bring forth" life on behalf of the sons of God.

Later that night, the Lord had me reading Ezra chapter 3 about the beginning of the Temple Restoration. As I read this passage, the Lord showed me that the High Priests Joshua and Zerubbabel had gathered other priests to help them begin the work of completing the building of the third temple in Israel. The first thing they did was to establish the foundations for an altar to the Lord in Jerusalem. They celebrated the Feast of Booths and had permission from Cyrus to bring cedarwood from the Sea of Joppa to build the foundations of the temple. Oh, how I love how the Lord's revelations are like puzzle pieces. Looking back, I see how they all fit together, but at the time, I had no idea where He was going with the puzzle pieces I had.

The next few nights, the Lord had me deep in studying the story that revolved around the rebuilding of the third temple. He led me to several passages that spoke of the same story which included Ezra chapters 5 and 6, Nehemiah, and Zechariah 3. He also led me to Isaiah 9:6 which says, "*Unto us a child is born, unto us a son is given. And the government shall rest upon His shoulders.*" Boldly, the word "government" stood out. As I reflected upon it, I saw the Lord standing tall and saw the government like a beautiful mantle draped over His shoulders. Questions broke forth in my mind.

What are the kingdom coverings, garments, mantles that we are given?

How are we to "put on", "be clothed in", or "robed" in these various garments?

Are there garments that are not of the Kingdom of God that we are to take off?

It occurred to me that garments are part of the form or appearance of the Bride, the priest, and the sons of God. As I brought these questions before the Lord, He led me to Ezekiel 42. In this chapter, the Lord instructs the priests on garments and defines that they were to enter into the inner courts in linen. When they left the inner courts to go out to the people, they were to change and leave their garments inside the Temple. This left me with one more pressing question, *"Lord, do garments need to be put on to release the spiritual disciplines?"* As I asked the question a prayer rose to my lips in regards to spiritual matters, *"I take off the garments of "desolation", "barrenness", and "not being sought after". I put on the bridal veil and the veil of being married to the Lord and sought after.*" That prayer caused a powerful shift between the heavens and the earth and the very next morning the miracles began.

14

WHAT IS KINGDOM LIVING?

"Jesus also said, 'This is what the kingdom of God is like. A man scatters seed on the ground. Night and day, whether he sleeps or gets up, the seed sprouts and grows, though he does not know how. All by itself the soil produces grain—first the stalk, then the head, then the full kernel in the head. As soon as the grain is ripe, he puts the sickle to it, because the harvest has come.'" Mark 4:26-29

You are the sons/daughters of the Living God. You are a Kingdom of priests. You are the Bride of Christ, and you are a mighty warrior in the Kingdom of God. It is time for us to stop living with a worldly mindset and train ourselves in Kingdom living. Don't you see, the day of the Lord is a day where we shall no longer see our Lord through a veil. We shall hear the voice of God clearly as He utters one final statement to the world, "I alone am God!" In that moment, His wrath is finished and comes to an end. His coming is a promise that shall suddenly appear like a thief in the night with majestic signs, wonders, and miracles. We are assured of His coming and we shall behold Him with awestruck wonder. These signs shall not go unnoticed, like a flashing beacon every eye shall see them. For

God's enemies will be completely destroyed along with all those who have refused to repent and turn to Him. But who will heed their warning? When the signs are posted, who will go the right direction and get ready so as to be prepared for the coming of Christ?

You are called to be prepared!

Understanding Kingdom living begins by defining kingdoms. Scripture tells us that there are two kingdoms at war. *"For behold, darkness covers the earth, and thick darkness is over the peoples; but the LORD will rise upon you, and His glory will appear over you." (Isaiah 60:2)* One of these kingdoms is the heavenly Kingdom. The Kingdom of God was created by the Lord God Almighty who created the heavens and the earth and all that is in them. *(Genesis 1,2; Nehemiah 9:6; Isaiah 45:7; Acts 17:24)* The other is the kingdom of earth inhibited by mankind, and presently under the rule of the Devil. The Devil, that ancient foe who was cast from the heavenly domain because he said in his heart, "*I will ascend to the throne and be like the Most High.*" Colossians 1:13 says, "*For He has rescued us from the dominion of darkness and brought us into the kingdom of the Son he loves".* What do we know about the Kingdom of God?

We know, "*His Kingdom is not a matter of talk but of power." (2 Corinthians 4:20)* Everything on earth shown to us in Scripture is an image and exact replica of the Kingdom of heaven. What are some of the replications? One of the first replications we see is the Tabernacle. The Tabernacle was the temporary structure Israel was commanded to build as a place to worship the Lord as they were wandering in the desert. "*And all this time our ancestors had a tent shrine for true worship, made to the exact specifications God provided to Moses." (Acts 7:47-50)* We also see imagery in

Scripture of where the Lord dwells, where He has His Courts and Heavenly throne room. These descriptions are in the Books of Job, Zechariah, and Revelation. What is His heavenly abode like? These Books tell us of the four living creatures, the Elders, the Seven Spirits of God and the myriads of myriads of angels.

Is the Kingdom of God just a place we are to dream about going once we leave this earth? In Luke 17:21, Jesus says, *"For the Kingdom of God is already among you. No longer will people say, 'Look here or look there.' For the Kingdom of God is within you."* If the Kingdom of God is within you, do you know how to access it? Out of fear, the Church has not taught us how to truly access it. Would it make you mad to know the enemy has access? Those who serve Satan know how to access it. Yet, the Church has kept you from tangibly understanding how to do so. Learning to access the Kingdom of God here on earth starts by understanding who you are in Christ and how to live with a Kingdom mindset. What do we need to do to get ready for Kingdom living? There are five stages of transformation that occur in increasing intensity as we grow in our newly transformed life.

Stage 1: A New Creation in Christ: In this first stage, we learn what it is to live. We set a firm foundation by being in the Word and prayer and learning to draw near to the Lord while also learning to pour out what we receive from Him unto others.

> *"Sharing in His death by our baptism means that we were co-buried with Him, so that when the Father's glory raised Christ from the dead, we were also raised with Him. We have been co-resurrected with Him so that we could be empowered to walk in the freshness of new life." (Romans 6:4)*

> *"He alone makes us adequate ministers who are focused on an entirely new covenant. Our ministry is not based on the letter of the law but through the power of the Spirit. The letter of the law kills, but the Spirit pours out life." (2 Corinthians 3:6)*
>
> *"When your self life craves the things that offend the Holy Spirit, you hinder Him from living free within you! And the Holy Spirit's intense cravings hinder your self-life from dominating you! So then, the two incompatible and conflicting forces within you are your self-life of the flesh and the new creation life of the Spirit. (Galatians 5:17)*
>
> *"Whether a man is circumcised or uncircumcised is meaningless to me. What really matters is the transforming power of this new creation life." (Galatians 6:15)*

Stage 2: Becoming A Royal Priesthood: In this stage we begin to learn what it means to come into a mutual relationship with the Lord. To obey, serve, and love. It entails learning to give, but also learning to receive from Him.

> *"But you are God's chosen treasure-a royal priesthood who are kings, a spiritual "nation" set apart as God's devoted ones. He called you out of darkness to experience His marvelous light, and now He claims you as His very own, so that you may declare His glories." (1 Peter 2:9)*
>
> *"Death once held us in its grip, and by the blunder of one man, death reigned as king over humanity. But now, how much more are we held in the grip of grace and continue reigning as kings in life, enjoying our regal freedom through*

the gift of perfect righteousness in the one and only Jesus, the Messiah." (Romans. 5:17)

Stage 3: Chosen of God: In this stage we go from a state of awareness about our identity to learning to walk in competence.

"But we ought always to thank God for you, brothers and sisters loved by the Lord, because God chose you as first fruits to be saved through the sanctifying work of the Spirit and through belief in the truth. He called you to this through our gospel, that you might share in the glory of our Lord Jesus Christ." (2 Thessalonians 2:13)

"Paul, a servant of God and an apostle of Jesus Christ to further the faith of God's elect and their knowledge of the truth that leads to godliness— in the hope of eternal life, which God, who does not lie, promised before the beginning of time, and which now at his appointed season he has brought to light through the preaching entrusted to me by the command of God our Savior," (Titus 1:1)

Stage 4: We have the Fullness of Christ: As we grow in competence, we also grow in our confidence. We learn to exercise our authority in both the spiritual as well as the physical realms.

"For in Christ all the fullness of the Deity lives in bodily form, and in Christ you have been brought to fullness. He is the head over every power and authority." (Colossians 2:9-10)

"And to know this love that surpasses knowledge—that you may be filled to the measure of all the fullness of God." (Ephesians 3:19)

"Until we all reach unity in the faith and in the knowledge of the Son of God and become mature, attaining to the whole measure of the fullness of Christ." (Ephesians 4:13)

Stage 5: We are the Sons of the Living God: As our confidence grows, we step into Kingdom Living and exercise our Kingdom rights and privileges in all the realms. We learn to go boldly into His throne room, and we learn to reign with Him and pour out His riches and glory.

"All creation waits in hopeful expectation for the revealing of the Sons of God." (Romans 8:19)

"And you are heirs of the prophets and of the covenant God made with your fathers. He said to Abraham, 'Through your offspring all peoples on earth will be blessed." (Acts 3:25)

"In the very place where it was said to them, 'You are not my people,' there they will be called 'children of the living God.'" (Romans 9:26)

"So, in Christ Jesus you are all children of God through faith, for all of you who were baptized into Christ have clothed yourselves with Christ." (Galatians 3:26-27)

Therefore, because of who we are in Christ we can live in Him!

> *"For to be sure, He was crucified in weakness, yet He lives by God's power. Likewise, we are weak in Him, yet by God's power we live with Him to serve you." (2 Corinthians 13:3-4)*

The Lord has given us authority and the fullness of Christ to put to use the weapons of divine power we have in Him. All these weapons the early church called spiritual disciplines. *"The Word of God is not imprisoned." (2 Timothy 2:9)* and "*our weapons of warfare are not of this world but of divine power to tear down strongholds." (2 Corinthians 10:4)* Therefore, we must be "disciplined" every day to put these things into practice and allow the Lord to train us in a living mindset. I will be honest; I don't have all the answers, but I know the One who does. Each of us has a unique job in this war and it is the Lord's job as our Commanding Officer and King to train us individually and collectively to do what He has called us to do. These weapons I am sharing with you are ones He has revealed to me in His Word and I am sharing how He has taught me to use them. But you are responsible to pray and seek God and ask Him how He desires you to put these weapons to use.

15

ACCESSING THE REALM OF HEAVEN

"But seek first the kingdom of God and his righteousness, and all these things will be added to you." Matthew 6:33

"He said to me, 'What do you see?' And I said, 'I see, and behold, a lampstand all of gold with its bowl on the top of it, and its seven lamps on it with seven spouts belonging to each of the lamps which are on the top of it; also two live trees by it, one on the right side of the bowl and one on the left side.' Then I said, to the angel who was speaking with me saying, 'What are these, my lord?' So the angel who was speaking with me answered and said to me, 'Do you not know what these are?' And I said, 'No my lord.' Then he said to me, 'This is the Word of the Lord to Zerubbabel saying, 'Not by might nor by power, but by My Spirit,' says the Lord of hosts." (Zechariah 4:2-6)

The Book of Zechariah paints a beautiful depiction of the seven-fold Spirit of the Lord. Before the throne of God, there is a golden bowl. In it is a menorah with the seven lamps representing the seven-fold Holy Spirit. Beside the bowl are the two olive trees. One on the right and one on the left. The roots of the trees drain olive oil into the golden bowl.

Is accessing the spiritual realms really that difficult? The first thing you must understand is that there is a connection between your spiritual and physical bodies. We have both. God created us with both a physical and a spiritual body. They are meant to be one and in their final state, we understand them as our "resurrected body in Christ". Do our bodies need to separate when we are accessing the spiritual realm? I believe the answer to this is no.

As we begin to pray and enter boldly before His throne, we will find there are hindrances to accessing the realm of Heaven. If access can be gained through spiritual disciplines, could it be that idols keep us from engaging in spiritual disciplines, thus limiting our access? When we fail to put these disciplines into practice, it negatively affects not only our spiritual body and health but our physical as well? Is complete health attainable? Could the cure to most health issues be as easy as confession, repentance, and engaging in spiritual disciplines on a regular basis? Now, I have to put a disclaimer here. This book and the methods taught are not a guarantee for healing. But in faith, we BELIEVE that as we draw upon the power of the Holy Spirit, we shall be healed. That we shall rise up to be the Bride, the priests, and the sons that He has created us to be.

Kingdom Living is about relationship. This is the day your relationship with the Lord begins anew. As you begin to surrender your will to His, you will find all that He has done for you and all that He has prepared for you. You will discover His house and His courts and He will teach you to be a keeper of His house and courts. I look forward to continuing this journey together.

Dear Reader,

In closing, it is my passion to help others learn creative ways to develop their faith. You can utilize further resources for growing your faith on through spiritual formation at: KingdomLivingWithJessie.com.

On the site, I put out a wealth of videos to help every believer to develop spiritual formation strategies in their life. I do two weekly shows on the website. The first, called "Rise Up" is a show designed to equip you in the process of spiritual formation. The second, called "Riding the Storms" is a show that teaches you how to apply Biblical truths as you navigate the challenges, trials, and storms in life.

I currently offer three courses designed to give you the foundational groundings of Biblical truths and the spiritual grounding you need to live the new life that is yours in our Lord and Savior Jesus Christ.

1) "Foundations of Kingdom Living": is all about advancing your faith to the place where you are walking in your Kingdom purpose while living in your God given authority.
2) “Rise of The Righteous” is geared to teach you about the authority you have been given and how one begins to live it out.
3) “Beautifully Adorned” focuses on spiritual and physical healing and walking in the fullness of authority by healing the sick, raising the dead, cleansing the lepers, rebuking demons, and living in the greater than these miracles the Lord has prepared in advance for us to do.

May you be blessed and may your faith be like a fire rolling over the multiple mountain tops.

Blessings,

Jessie Czebotar

Printed in Great Britain
by Amazon

52671316R00066